Practical

EASTER

(Québec and the Maritimes)

1992

Hayit Publishing

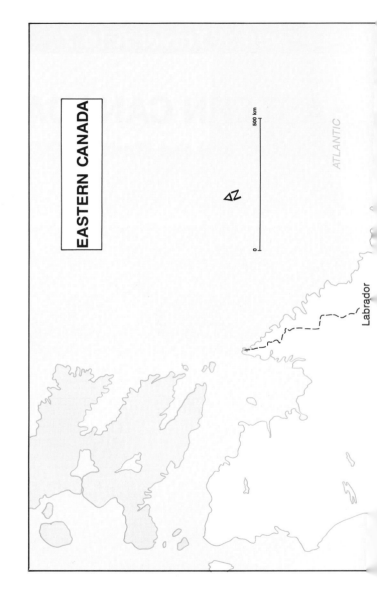

EASTERN CANADA

Labrador

ATLANTIC

0 — 500 km

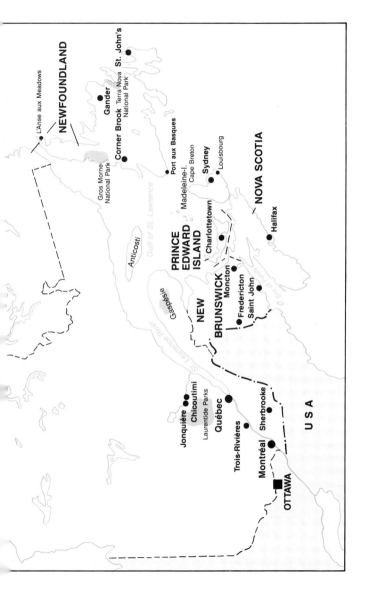

<1st> Edition 1992

UK Edition: ISBN 1 874251 20 7
US Edition: ISBN 1 56634 007 1

© copyright 1992 UK Edition: Hayit Publishing GB, Ltd, London
                 US Edition: Hayit Publishing USA, Inc., New York

© copyright 1991 original version: Hayit Verlag GmbH, Cologne/Germany

Author: Jo Bentfeld
Translation, Adaption, Revision: Scott Reznik
Print: Druckhaus Rombach, Freiburg/Germany
Photography: Tourist Office of Québec, Düsseldorf, Tourist Office of Canada, Frankfurt; Thomas Stankiewicz
Distribution to the trade:
  UK: Amalgamated Book Service/Kent
  USA: National Book Network/Lanham, MD

Using this Book

Books in the series *Practical Travel A to Z* offer a wealth of practical information. You will find the most important tips for your travels conveniently arranged in alphabetical order. Cross-references aid in orientation so that even entries which are not covered in depth, for instance ''Holiday Apartments,'' lead you to the appropriate entry, in this case ''Accommodation.'' Thematically altered entries are also cross-referenced. For example, under the heading ''Medication,'' there appear the following references: ''Medical Care,'' ''Travel Medications,'' ''Pharmacies,'' ''Vaccinations.''

With travel guides from the series *Practical Travel A to Z* the information is already available before you depart on your trip. Thus, you are already familiar with necessary travel documents and maps, even customs regulations. Travel within the country is made easier through comprehensive presentation of public transportation and car rentals in addition to the practical tips ranging from medical assistance to newspapers available in the country. The descriptions of cities are arranged alphabetically as well and include the most important facts about the particular city, its history and a summary of significant sights. In addition, these entries include a wealth of practical tips — from shopping, restaurants and accommodation to important local addresses. Background information does not come up short either. You will find interesting information about the people and their culture as well as the regional geography, history and the current political and economic situation.

As a particular service to our readers, *Practical Travel A to Z* includes prices in hard currencies so that they might gain a more accurate impression of prices even in countries with high rates of inflation. Most prices quoted in this book have been converted to US$ and £.

Contents

Acadia

Acadia is the historical term for the original French settlements on Canada's northern Atlantic coast, presently located in the State of Maine, the provinces of New Brunswick and Nova Scotia. The French monarch staked a claim on this portion of land because the French captain and explorer Jacques Cartier from Saint-Malo had explored and mapped the western Atlantic coast in the years 1534/1535 and 1541, commissioned by the French King François I.

The French sovereignty gradually lost in the constant struggle between England and France for the control over North America. With France's defeat in the Seven Years' War from 1756 to 1763, France ceded the last of its North American possessions in the Treaty of Paris. Only the small independent colony Saint Pierre et Miquelon was overlooked by England's negotiators, and for this reason, it is still a departement of France today. Both of the two larger islands only encompass 242 square kilometres and can be reached by ferry departing from Fortune. The designation for this region (which is derived from the classical ''Acadia'' of the antique) was carried over to the French settlers living in this region. The Acadians still lead a culturally distinctive lifestyle within the multicultural Canadian society. Recognised officially, their flag symbolises their autonomy. Even without a special occasion, one can see the French Tricolour flown above Acadian villages in Nova Scotia, for example. Only when closely scrutinised will one discover the golden star in the first broad stripe: Stella Maris, the star of Mary, the mother of God, patron saint of the Catholic Acadians.

Air Travel → *Travelling to Eastern Canada / By Air*

Accommodation

Bed & Breakfast: growing increasingly popular in Canada is this type of accommodation which offers the opportunity to establish interesting contacts with other guests or even the family running the establishment. There are, however, B&B's which are run more like guest houses or small hotels and lack the original familiar atmosphere. The prices for a room in a Bed & Breakfast vary greatly, as one might expect. A single room will usually cost between 25 and 35 Canadian dollars and a double, 40 to 50 Canadian dollars. Breakfast is usually included in the price, but not always. Sometimes a charge of 4 or 5 Canadian dollars is added. Frequently, other meals are available in some of the bed and breakfasts, and one can even take part in the hosts' meals in some cases. Information and lists of the B&B's are available from the Tourist Information Offices in each province *(→Tourist Information)*.

Campsites: *→Camping*

Youth Hostels: The youth hostels are the least expensive type of accommodation in Canada, but are not widely represented. With an international youth hostel card, one can stay overnight in the hostels for 5 to 15 Canadian dollars. Information and the Canadian Hostelling Association register is available through youth hostel organisations in your home country or by contacting: The Canadian Hostelling Association, 333 River Road, Vanier City, Ottawa, Ontario, K1L 8B9. Similar lodging is offered by the YMCA and YWCA, which are represented in every larger city. These often meet hotel standards and are more expensive than youth hostels (single rooms between 20 and 28 Canadian dollars). A comprehensive list is available through: Central YMCA, 20 Grosvenor St., Toronto, M4Y 1A8.

Hotels/Motels: In Canada, one will have no difficulty finding a hotel or motel. They are generally well equipped according to North American standards. Prices range from 40 to 70 Canadian dollars in smaller towns and from 70 to 150 Canadian dollars per night in the larger cities. Of course, one can probably also find less expensive lodgings, but rooms can cost in excess of 150 Canadian dollars as well. The prices are not quoted for a single or double room, but as a base price for the room in general. For additional guests, at least 5 Canadian dollars, but usually 10% of the base price is added. Breakfast is hardly ever included in the price. One should take advantage of the special weekend rates offered by many of the larger hotels. The rates are frequently 50% less expensive.

The Appalachians

The Appalachians are one of the oldest mountain ranges in the world. Today, they have long since been eroded to a sub-alpine mountain range. Somewhat younger than the northern Laurentian range, these mountains encompass the eastern portion of the United States and extend along the coast to the north, gradually losing altitude. In Canada, the area from the Maritimes to the St. Lawrence River belongs to this mountain region: the islands are the last of the foothills: after these, the mountain range sinks into the Atlantic. The southern portion of Québec south of the St. Lawrence River is part of this region: the Gaspésie.

The Appalachians are considered to be rich in natural resources of all sorts. They are, however, not suited for agriculture. The humus layer in some of the valleys is sufficient to support orchards, however, this region is mainly used in forestry. For this reason, huge areas south of the St. Lawrence basin have remained forest wilderness.

Automobile Clubs

European automobile clubs have a cooperative agreement with the Canadian automobile club CAA, the Canadian Automobile Association. The representative offices can be found in the telephone books under this name. In remote areas, however, these offices are few and far between. The police are very helpful, though, and can be reached by dialling '0.' The operator will then connect you with the police station in charge. Furthermore, helping out is an unwritten law in such regions, which is applicable to foreign guests as well as residents. In case of a break-down, it is customary to signal for help with a white cloth attached to the window.

Bay of Fundy

The Nova Scotia province is connected with the neighbouring province of New Brunswick by a small isthmus on which the city of Amherst, Nova Scotia is located. A massive Atlantic inlet, the *Bay of Fundy* reaching far into the land, separates the two Canadian provinces. On its southern inlet, the bay is around 100 kilometres wide, opening to the ocean. It extends almost 150 kilometres to the north continually decreasing in width. The peninsula *Chignecto* then divides the bay into two sounds. To the south, the *Minas Basin* extends another 100 kilometres into Nova Scotia; to the north, the *Chignecto Bay* separates the two provinces for another 75 kilometres, ending near Amherst. What is special about the Bay of Fundy is the natural spectacle of the tides which can be observed from continually new and different perspectives when travelling around the bay. The difference between high and low tide is more extreme here than anywhere else on the globe: during the extremes, a difference of 16.6 vertical metres can be measured. The cause of this is the bay's funnel shape described above. The masses of water flowing into the bay increase in depth as the coast decreases in width, until every corner of the bay reaches its highest water level. A further characteristic of this natural spectacle is the *tidal bore,* the tidal turning point with which the high tide washes back into the bay. At first, the water recedes leaving regions along the coast dry as far as one can see. One can then hike on the floor of the bay, boats in the harbour and along the shore lay on their sides. The mass of water flowing into the bay meets with the undertow, causing it to rush over the outflowing tide. At first, this shallow wall of water, only a hand's width, then wanders into the basin, continually increasing in height until the water reaches a height of several metres finally breaking at the mouths of the rivers.

During low tide, the river inlets run dry, ponds and rivers drain into the bay's basin. With the sudden tidal shift, the tidal bore breaks into the inlet bringing about a turn of events: the water flows back into the interior basin. The *Saint John River* near Saint John, New Brunswick offers a spectacular vantage point for observing this natural phenomenon. Here, one can also see the famous *Reversing Falls,* resulting from the tidal bore. During low tide, the powerful river flows over a mountain ledge and plunges five metres into the harbour basin of Saint John. When high tide returns, the falls are reversed, the water gushing upstream over the rapids. The effects of the tides can be observed as far as Fredericton, the capital of New Brunswick, over 100 kilometres upstream from Saint John.

The *Flowerpots* are yet another attraction resulting from the tides. These are rock formations along the shores of the bay of Fundy. During high tide, one sees small islands in the water covered with trees and shrubs. Only during low tide is the lower part of these formations visible: the base of these islands has been worn down to a stem by the perpetual action of the tides. The image of a wine glass made of stone and filled with plants is unmistakable. These ''flowerpots'' can be admired up-close by hiking out into the basin during low tide. At the mouth of Chignecto Bay, *Fundy National Park* stretches along the northern shores in New Brunswick around Alma. This park is only 206 square kilometres and serves to preserve the typical coastal formations along the shore, carved over the centuries by the tidal currents. At the foot of the rock formations, one can hike along the coast in the basin during low tide. The most beautiful flowerpots, however, are found further north at the end of Chignecto Bay near Cape Hopewell at the mouth of the Petitcodiac River. Information: Fundy National Park, Alma NB E0A 1B0, Tel: (506) 887-2000.

Spectacular results of the tides can also be observed along the coast of Nova Scotia. Especially worth seeing is the Minas Basin and its strait near Cape Split, where the tide reaches its highest point. Also, *Digby Gut,* the narrow canal connecting the Annapolis Basin with the Bay of Fundy, is by all means worth a visit.

Buses →*Transportation in Eastern Canada*

Business Hours

Most businesses are open Monday to Saturday from 9:30 am to 6 pm. Grocery stores are frequently open longer. Department stores and shopping centres in the large cities are open Thursdays and Fridays until 9 pm and are often open on Sundays as well. Supermarkets are open seven days a week from 7 am, closing at 6 pm and 5 pm during weekends. In larger cities, they are open on Thursdays and Fridays until 9 pm.

Canada's rivers and lakes are ideal for canoeists

Banks are open Monday to Friday from 10 am to 3 pm, Thursdays until 6 pm.
Post Offices are open Monday to Friday from 8 am to 5 pm and are sometimes
even open on Saturdays, either during the morning or the entire day.

Camping

Especially in Canada, a motor caravan, camper or tent can be highly recommended. It is not explicitly prohibited to camp in the wilderness, but it is unusual
because there are a sufficient number of campsites.

Canada has excellent private campsites as well as outstanding public campsites located within the national parks. The facilities are good to excellent.
Most of the campsites are open from June to September/October. Advance
notification of arrival is, however, only advisable for the national parks along
the coast. Not all campsites accept reservations.

Information is available at the information offices in your home country or in
Canada *(→Tourist Information)*. In addition, there are three organisations in
Québec which will send lists of campsites or can help with other inquiries:

Camping and Caravaning
Fédération québécoise de camping et de caravaning, 4545, avenue Pierre de
Coubertin, C.P. 1000, succursale "M" Montreal (Québec)
Canoeing and Camping
Fédération québécoise du canot-camping (address: see above)
Outdoor Centre
Réseau Plein Air (address: see above)

Canada

The federal state of Canada extends across the northern part of the American
Continent between the Atlantic and the Pacific. Its name resulted from a
misunderstanding: the first Frenchmen to arrive in Canada asked the original
Indian inhabitants in sign language where they had landed. The answer was:
Kanatta — the usual term for village or settlement in the Algonkin family of
languages.

Canada has been an independent federal state since 1867 under the representative sovereignty of the English monarchy. The English monarchs are,
therefore, the heads of state and are represented by a governor general appointed by the king or queen.

The Canadian Federation is made up of ten individual provinces as well as two territories with restricted autonomy. The latter are the Yukon Territory and the Northwest Territories; the former are (from west to east) the provinces of British Columbia, Alberta, Saskatchewan, Manitoba, Ontario, Québec, New Brunswick, Nova Scotia, Newfoundland and Prince Edward Island.

The area of Canada encompasses around 10 million square kilometres. The population, in contrast, numbers only 25 million.

Cape Breton Highlands National Park

Located on the island of Cape Breton (Nova Scotia) and measuring almost 1000 square kilometres, this national park is a paradise for nature lovers. The rugged coastal landscape and the unsettled highlands are definitely similar to the Scottish regions which inspired the park's name. On the plateau (360 metres above sea-level) is composed of an conglomeration of tundra, lakes and swamps: a rare geographical composition with an attraction all its own. The NS route no. 19 loops through the park, marked as ''Cabot Trail'' on the western, eastern and northern sides. The Cabot Trail is a stretch of approximately 300 kilometres of basic highway. At regular intervals, there are a total of ten public campgrounds run by the park administration. Hiking paths lead from every campground through the mountain forests up the slopes to the plateau which has an altitude of 532 metres above sea level at its highest elevation. More than 200 kilometres of hiking paths as well as the chain of rivers, ponds and lakes make this park a unique experience for nature lovers, who will frequently encounter black bears, lynx, red deer and elk.

Accommodation in a sufficient number of hotels and motels is available in almost a dozen small coastal towns.

Cape Breton Highlands / **Practical Information**
Campsites
Arichat: ''Acadian Campsite,'' Box 24, NS B0E 1A0, Tel: 226-2447, open from May 15 to October 15.

Baddeck: ''Bras d'Or Lakes Campground,'' located on the Bras d'Or lake, Tel: 295-2329 or 295-3467, open June 1 to September 30.

Cheticamp: ''Plage Saint Pierre Campground,'' Box 430, NS B0E 1H0, Tel: 224-2112, open from June to October.

Ingonish Beach: "Ingonish Campground," Cape Breton Highlands National Park, Tel: 285-2329, open June 25 to September 4.

Louisbourg: "Louisbourg Motorhome Park," Box 8, NS B0A 1M0, no telephone, open from June 1 to September 30.

Margaree Forks: "Buckles Trailer Court and Campsite," NS B0E 2A0, open from May to October

Hotels

Arichat: "L'Auberge Acadienne"***, High Road, Box 59, NS B0E 1A0, Tel: 226-2200, open all year, renovated in the style of the 19th century, 17 rooms with bath, singles Can\$ 49, doubles Can\$ 55-60, children under ten free, restaurant.

Baddeck: "Inverary Inn Resort"****, located at exit number 8 to route 205 and Shore Road, Tel: 295-2674, open all year, 166 motel units, 9 cottages all equipped with bath, singles Can\$ 45-80, doubles Can\$ 55-100, restaurant.

In Fundy National Park, one has an excellent view of the natural spectacle brought about by the tides

''Cozy Motel and Lodge''**, Shore Road, Box 505, NS B0E 1B0, Tel: 295-2195, open from June to October, singles Can$ 65, doubles Can$ 70, children under 5 free, breakfast, restaurant.

''The Point Bed & Breakfast,'' 4 Twinning Street, NS B0E 1B0, Tel:295-3368, open from June to October, 3 rooms, no smoking, singles and doubles Can$ 30-55.

Cheticamp: ''Laurie's Motel,'' Main street, Box 1, NS B0E 1H0, Tel: 224-2400, open all year, 55 motel units with bath/shower, radio, television, telephone, some with balconies, singles Can$ 48-65, doubles Can$ 55-75, children under 12 free.

Ingonish: ''The Island Inn,'' Box 116, NS B0C 1L0, Tel: 285-2404, open from January to March and from May to November, 11 rooms, 8 with their own bath, all with radio and television, television in the lounge, singles Can$ 25-40, doubles Can$ 30-45, children under 2 free, under 12 Can$ 3.

Louisbourg: ''Greta Cross Bed & Breakfast,'' 81 Pepperell Street, Box 153, NS B0A 1M0, Tel: 733-2833, open from March to November, 3 rooms, two of which share a bath, breakfast, singles Can$ 25, doubles Can$ 30, children under 5 free.

Margaree Harbour: ''Whale Cove Summer Village''***, 4 kilometres south of Margaree Harbour on route 219, Tel: 235-2202, open from May to October, 30 summer houses with bath/WC, television and telephone, one bedroom Can$ 50-65, two bedrooms Can$ 60-75.

Sydney: ''Auberge Wandlyn Inn''***, 100 Kings Road, NS B1S 1A1, Tel: 539-3700, open all year, newly renovated, 50 rooms and mini-suites with bath, Can$ 50-90, children free, restaurant.

''Keltic Motel''**, 294 Keltic Drive, Sydney River, NS B1R 1V7, Tel: 562-3111, open all year, 10 units, 2 with a kitchen, all with bath, singles Can$ 37-40, doubles Can$ 40-43.

Information: Superintendent Cape Breton Highlands National Park, Ingonish Beach, NS B0C 1L0, Tel: (902) 285-2270.

Restaurants

Baddeck: ''Bell Buoy Seafood & Steak Restaurant,'' Chebucto Street, NS B0E 1B0. Fish specialities, steaks, appetisers, salads and desserts. Children's menu available. Open from June to October.

Cheticamp: ''Parkview Motel Dining Room and Lounge,'' Box 117, NS B0E 1H0, Tel: 224-3232 and 224-2596. Located at the entrance to the national park about

4.8 kilometres west of Cheticamp. The seafood, steaks, pastries and homemade bread are highly recommended. Open from May to October.

Glace Bay: "Mike's Lunch," 4A Sterling Road, NS B1A 3X3, Tel: 849-1010. Restaurant and snack bar. Fish dishes, steaks, homemade soups, Italian dishes, salads and sandwiches. Breakfast is also served here. Open all year.

Louisbourg: "Fleur-de-Lis Dining Room," 1225 Main Street, NS B0A 1M0, Tel: 733-2844. Very nice restaurant, specialising in the preparation of all types of seafood. Open from June to October.

Margaree Harbour: "Marion Elizabeth Schooner Restaurant," Margaree Harbour, across from an old schooner, Tel: 235-2317. The fish dishes, sandwiches and the continually freshly baked cakes can be especially recommended. A pianist provides the proper atmosphere. Open from June to October.

Margaree Valley: "The Normaway Inn," located between N.E. Margaree and Lake O'Law, Tel: 248-2987. One should definitely try the salmon and mussel dishes! In addition, lamb, vegetarian and herb dishes are among the selection. Very good selection of wines. Open from June to October.

North Sydney: "Clansman Motel Dining Room," Peppet St., Box 216, NS B2A 3M3, Tel: 794-7226. Good home cooking, reasonable princes. Children's menu. Open all year.

Car Rental and Purchase

Almost all of the rental car agencies are located in the airports or train stations. The most significant companies are: Avis, Budget, Hertz, Tilden and Via Route. One must expect to pay about Can$ 40 per day. The advantage from renting from one of the larger chains is that one can rent the vehicle at one location and return it elsewhere. This service is, however, not always free of charge.

If travelling from Europe, it is generally less expensive to book a rental car from Europe. This is also true for the abundant mobile homes and RV's (recreational vehicles).

Most companies will not rent a vehicle to persons under 25. In addition, one must be aware that it is not possible to rent a vehicle in Canada without a credit card.

The full liability insurance, which costs extra, should only be refused if one is prepared to accept the risk!

Purchasing a vehicle is commonly chosen as an alternative when travelling in Canada. It is important to buy a vehicle that is still registered and insured because these formalities can only be taken care of if one has a permanent address in Canada. Therefore, it is necessary to buy a car from a private party or dealer who is willing to assume the responsibility of registering and insuring the vehicle. One should definitely put the authorisation of use into writing. At some dealers, it is possible to put a clause into the contract guaranteeing that the dealer will purchase back the vehicle. One must then drive back to the point of departure at the end of one's holidays.

Charlottetown

Charlottetown (population: approximately 16,000) is the only city and the largest settlement on Prince Edward Island, as well as being a university town and the governmental seat. The city's natural settings made it nothing short of ideal for building a harbour. Together with the access to the ocean, three rivers (*North* or *York River*, *East* or *Hillsborough River* and *West River*) form an intersecting waterway. The city and harbour lie on the northern junction of these rivers. These bodies of water are only actually rivers in their upper courses. About half way to Charlottetown, they broaden to become wide and elongated bays. The capital obtains its charm by the unusual mixture of small town houses and monumental buildings in the English style from the past century, which is certainly not expected so close to the neighbouring wooden, half-timbered and brick houses. The old churches, governmental and administrative buildings seem to have taken on dimensions too large for this small city. The city administration has prohibited high rise buildings so that the original character of this settlement has remained virtually unchanged.

Charlottetown / **Sights**

The *Fort Amherst National Historic Park* is located directly south of the city, on the left bank of the entrance to the bay. Here, the settlement of Prince Edward Island began 270 years ago. The historical outdoor museum preserves the recollection of the Franco-Canadian settlement of Port La Joye as well as the English fortress complex which was established later. Built on this strategically perfect site, *Fort Amherst* guarded the narrower entrance to the broad lagoon of Charlottetown Harbour.

The *Province House* on Confederation Plaza captivates through its clear architectural lines and its unpretentious appearance. The "Fathers of the Confederation" once convened here, establishing Canada over 100 years ago. The
interior is preserved in its original style and upholds the memory of the 23
delegates who assembled here in 1864.

The massive *Confederation Centres of the Arts,* built 27 years ago stands in
contradiction with Charlottetown's small city atmosphere and is also an object of disagreement. The massive concrete construction, completed for the
100-year anniversary of the historical conference, is not to everyone's taste.
This building also houses a cultural centre.

The southern point of the peninsula with *Victoria Park* is another area worth
seeing. The old cannon barrels of Old Battery Point still stand threateningly
over the sound, guarding the waterway to the city and harbour as they did
200 years ago. From this vantage point, one has an especially nice view of
the lagoon and the strip of land on the opposite shores.

The *Lieutenant Governor's Residence* is located on the edge of the park in
the shade of the old trees. This building was built in colonial style using classic
columns, a style which can often be found on the American continent.

A tour through the city and harbour area can be taken independently; the
"Visitor Centre" will help by providing information. It is, however, also advisable
to take part in the free daily tours through the centre of the city, which begin
at the Province House mentioned above.

Charlottetown / **Practical Information**

Accommodation

Charlottetown offers a dozen *Hotels/Motels* with a large number of beds. Rooms
cost from Can$ 55 to Can$ 165.

In addition to the relatively small number of hotels, there are a number of *Tourist
Homes* and *Guest Houses.* This type of accommodation is relatively inexpensive. Listing these is not appropriate here because there are usually only a
limited number of rooms (one or two) offered by private parties. Rooms are
priced from Can$ 18.

The numerous *Campgrounds* also offer ample space during the season. These
campgrounds take measures to ensure high standards and the prices average
around Can$ 12 per night.

The only *Youth Hostel* on the island is located 5 kilometres north of the city on the outskirts: 153 Mt. Edward Road, Tel: (902) 894-9696. Members pay Can$ 8, non members, Can$ 10. The youth hostel is open from May 15 to September 1.

Information: Visitor information Centre, University Avenue, Royality Mall, Tel: (902) 892-2457. Here one can obtain the "Visitor's Guide," which lists accommodation alternatives, restaurants, shops and sights.

Special Events: *Old Home Week* during the middle of August; *Lobster Supper* in July and August. In addition, there are numerous festivals, folk celebrations, jamborees and parades all during the summer months.

In both of the theatres in the Confederation Centre, theatre performances, art exhibitions and concerts take place from mid June to the end of September. One should purchase tickets early enough.

The island of Cape Breton / Nova Scotia is reminiscent of the Scottish highlands, the inspiration behind the province's name

Clothing

In general, a normal travel wardrobe will suffice for Canada and the North American continent.

Those who travel through the wilderness should, however, pack additional equipment. In the interior and the north, one must be prepared for sudden changes in the weather, a few days of rain or cold wind. Those who would like to have appropriate clothing along but would also like to travel light will still need to take clothing appropriate for all types of weather.

Therefore, a recommendation that can also be found in the brochures for the northern national parks: Gore-Tex. The lightweight articles of clothing made from this waterproof material, which also allows for transpiration, are appropriate for a number of weather conditions — and protect against the mosquitoes as well! A long pair of trousers and a parka made from this material are the solution in every climatic situation.

Consulates

Those who encounter difficulties will only have one institution in the country to which they can turn: the embassy (addresses listed below). One can also contact the consuates in Eastern Canada. Regardless of the name of the institution, they will be willing to offer their help — given that there is an emergency — and this is, of course, checked beforehand.

Diplomatic Representation

United States:
100 Wellington Street
Ottawa K1P 5T1
Tel: (613) 238-5335
Fax: (613) 563-7701
United Kingdom:
80 Elgin Street
Ottawa K1P 5K7
Tel: (613) 237-1530
Fax: (613) 237-7980

Australia:
50 O'Connor Street
Ottawa K1P 6L2
Tel: (613) 236-0841
New Zealand:
Metropolitan House
99 Bank Street, Suite 727
Ottawa K1P 6G3
Tel: (613) 238-5991
Fax: (613) 238-5707

Credit Cards →*Modes of Payment*

Cuisine

"Normal" Canadian cuisine is very similar to the American. Average restaurants serve simple vegetable soups, green salad, beef and potatoes, fruit pies and ice cream. The Canadian cuisine, however, has made progress in this area. Canada offers international cuisine, a development which can be accredited to the numerous groups of immigrants.

In general, all of the salmon dishes can be recommended in Canada.

Every region is proud of their own specialties, which are truly delicacies. Along the coast, seafood including lobster is of course on many menus.

In the individual provinces, the residents are particularly proud of the following specialities:

New Brunswick: grilled salmon, "fiddleheads", dulse (edible seaweed), blueberry and rhubarb pie.

Newfoundland: cod prepared in a variety of ways, "seal flipper pie," a speciality that animal lovers will certainly forego, and bakeapple berries, rich in vitamin C.

Nova Scotia: Digby scallops, mussel soup. "Solomon Gundy," a stew made from herring and minced beef, marinated in vinegar, oil, onions and green pepper, blueberry and rhubarb pie, fresh strawberries and apple specialities.

Prince Edward Island: a number of excellent potato and vegetable dishes, Malpeque oysters and many types of cheeses.

Québec: Excellent French cuisine, all of the recipes that make use of maple syrup, "tourtière," a pastry filled with partridge, deer or rabbit and finely chopped potatoes, "cipaille," a pastry filled with venison and potatoes and cheese ("Er-mitle" and "Ricotta).

The Canadians are predominantly beer drinkers, but in recent years, the first-class wines grown on the Niagara peninsula and the Okanagan Valley are gaining popularity. Connoisseurs recommend the rye whiskey, which is of the highest quality. In Québec, one should try "caribou," a mixed drink made from red wine and hard liquor.

In restaurants that are not licensed to serve liquor *(→Restaurants),* tea is served in addition to a variety of soft drinks.

Currency

The unit of currency in Canada is the Canadian dollar (Can$), which is sub-divided into 100 cents. The dollar notes are in the denominations of 1, 2, 5, 10, 20, 50, 100, 500, and 1000 Can$. Coins are in 1, 5, 10, 25, and 50 cent denominations. They are called (in the listed order): copper (or penny), nickel, dime, quarter and half-dollar. The somewhat small dollar coins are rare. It is common practice to carry a role of one and two dollar notes. It is important to note that for telephone booths and public transportation, one should have an ample number of coins available (especially quarters), otherwise one will not be able to place a call or ride the bus since change is rarely available in these instances.

Foreign currencies may be taken in and out of the country in an unlimited amount.

→*Modes of Payment*

Customs Regulations

Visitors can bring all articles for personal use into Canada duty-free. If bring-ing in an expensive apparatus or items where it is not obvious that they will be taken back out of the country, it is possible that one must make a security deposit. Of course, this money is returned when leaving the country upon presenting the article.

Two widely used means of transportation in Canada: the light aircraft and the motor boat ▶

It is a good idea to bring along a receipt if bringing new or near new articles into the country — not because of the Canadian customs, but because of the customs when returning to one's home country.

Persons over 16 years of age may bring 200 cigarettes, 50 cigars or one kilogramme tobacco into Canada. One must be at least 19 years of age to bring 1.1 litres of spirits into Canada (18 years of age for Prince Edward Island and Québec). Luxury articles must, however, be declared when passing through customs. Plants and fresh agricultural products (fruit, vegetables and meat) may not be taken into Canada and pets may only be brought into the country with an import permit. For cats and dogs, vaccination certification is necessary, proving that the animal was vaccinated within the past 12 months and at least one month before entering Canada.

Hunting firearms (hand guns are illegal in Canada!) plus 200 rounds of ammunition may be brought into the country for personal use but should be transported in baggage only after having been dismantled.

Driving Licence →*Travel Documents*

Electricity

In Canada the electricity is alternating current, 110 volts and 60 Hz without exception.

One might need an adapter for appliances made for 220 volts; these must fit the North American norm. Adapters are available in most specialty shops. If the electrical appliance was not built for 110 volts then it must be switched to this voltage. Where this is not provided for — for instance with motor caravans and campers — one will need a transformer. These can also be purchased at specialty stores.

Embassies →*Consulates*
Entering Canada →*Travel Documents*

Fishing

Bringing along fishing gear can definitely be recommended. The wealth of fish in the creeks, rivers and lakes is indescribable (pike, trout, lake salmon, grayling and char) and those who enjoy eating fish fresh from the frying pan will certainly not be disappointed.

In Canada, everyone is permitted to fish; one merely needs a fishing licence which can be purchased in the sporting goods stores. One exception is New Brunswick, where citizens of foreign countries must go to the ministry. One should note that the licences are only valid for one province. Those who wish to fish in the national parks must buy a supplementary licence. In the provincial parks, the provincial licence is valid. It becomes somewhat more complicated in some of the provinces where the licences are subdivided into two categories; the general fishing licence and the supplementary licence permitting salmon fishing must be paid separately. Nothing can be done about this; one must be sure one has the proper licensing!

Only sport fishermen, who drop a line off the coast of the Maritimes (known for the huge schools of tuna in these waters) need no license.

Fortress of Louisbourg

There are a total of 82 historical sites in Canada which are run as outdoor museums and the most widely known among these is Fortress of Louisbourg. From Sydney on Cape Breton Island, the 35 kilometres on the NS Route 22 takes one back to the Middle Ages. This road is the only land route to this old French fortress. According to the Treaty of Utrecht, France had to relinquish Acadia and, thus, also Nova Scotia in 1713. Only Cape Breton Island remained under the power of the French. For this reason, this portion of Nova Scotia became the focus of French colonial politics.

In order to secure this area well into the future, the court of Versailles decided to build an unconquerable fortress in the same fashion as the famous Vauban complexes. Construction on the bastion surrounding the small, natural harbour of Louisbourg on the Atlantic coast of Cape Breton Island was already underway in 1719. The collosal project proved unsuccessful, however. After sums of money running into the millions were either pumped into the construction or diverted into various "open pockets" over 25 years, the uncompleted fortress including its underoccupied garrison fell into the hands of the Anglo-Americans for the first time in 1745. After only 45 days of occupation, the occupying forces surrendered the fortress. In 1748, in accordance with the treaty of Aachen, the fortress was given once again to France. However, it fell back to England ultimately in 1758.

As returning the fortress in 1748 caused a furious storm of protest in New England, the fortress was razed.

In 1961, the Federal Canadian Government in Ottawa decided to rebuild the fortress of Louisbourg as a museum. The goal was the complete reconstruction of the massive complex according to the original plans: seven fortification buildings and a total of 500 other buildings were to be rebuilt. A quarter of this challenge has been met; large portions of the complex have been completed at an expense of 30 million Canadian dollars to date. The reconstruction creates a significant number of jobs in a region with a traditionally high rate of unemployment. Each building within the 6,700 hectare large complex is built strictly according to the old plans: from the governor's palace to the fishermen's cottages.

Even more interesting for visitors to the Fortress of Louisbourg is the fact that the lively hubub of the middle ages is performed by the 400 present day residents of Louisbourg. In the summer, the number increases by a few hundred students. Then the newly built "old" walls are once again filled with life: the arsenals are guarded by soldiers in historical uniforms, protecting the city from any enemies approaching from the Atlantic. In the streets, the civilians hurry by in medieval costumes. In the ironsmith's shop, one hears the clang of the anvil, the cooper handcrafts vats and sawdust flies through the air at the carpenter's. These people are all working directly on the reconstruction project. Even the children in school or at play on the streets are dressed in the costumes of that time, and visitors are more than welcome to take a peek into the soup kettles of a family sitting down to the midday meal. Of course, this food is prepared according to Acadian recipes handed down over generations. In less than 15 minutes, the illusion is perfected: one believes to have travelled 250 years back in time.

Information: Fortress of Louisbourg, National Historic Park, Box 160, Louisbourg, NS B0A 1M0, Tel: (902) 733-2280.

Fredericton

The small provincial metropolis of Fredericton, New Brunswick (population: approximately 40,000), extends along both banks of the Saint John River. On the south bank is the centre of the city and it is connected to the other districts across the river by two automobile bridges.

Fredericton / **History**

Fredericton has only been settled since 1732. At that time, some of the Acadians moved here. They called the village "Pointe-Ste.-Anne." The families which settled here also fell victim to the persecution of Acadians beginning in 1755 *(→Acadia);* their houses were burned to the ground. The attempts to resettle were hindered by the hostile Micmac Indians. Only in 1768 could resettlement begin. Exiled loyalists settled here and the British government gave in to their desire to have their own colony. The settlement was then given its present-day name, after Frederic, one of King George III's sons.

Although it has become an administrative centre and almost a military post as well, Fredericton remains a small city. Administrative buildings and retirement homes make up the city's profile today.

The most famous outdoor museum in Canada: the Fortress of Louisbourg on Cape Breton Island

Fredericton / **Sights**

The cozy little residential city on the riverbanks has meanwhile acquired a series of impressive buildings which were built immediately after the founding of the administrative seat, some of which seem to be overproportioned. This is the case with the *Parliamentary Building* along the river, the *City Hall,* the *Judicial Building,* the bishop's cathedral, *Christ Church,* and the *Governor's Residence.* All of these buildings are built in the style of the Georgonian and Victorian regimes making them interesting reflections of this time. Belonging to these as well are the *Soldiers' Barracks* and the *Guard House* on the old parade square in the park which is now the location of a museum and a cultural centre.

Lord Beaverbock, a native of the province, contributed a great deal to the present appearance of the inner city with its boulevards lined with old elms. During World War II, he was a minister in Winston Churchill's military cabinet and as a newspaper magnate (editor of the ''Daily Express'' among other newspapers) responsible, as one might guess, for propoganda. He donated the beautiful *theatre* and an *art gallery* with an excellent collection of old masterpieces predominantly by English and American artists.

The city has been home to the *University of New Brunswick* since 1859. Those who wish to do so can supplement their impression of the city with a perspective from the river. A replica of a paddle wheel steamer, the ''Pioneer Princess II,'' departs on river tours daily from the Regent Street Wharf.

Fredericton / **Practical Information**

Accommodation

Bed & Breakfast: There is a large selection of B&B homes with nightly prices from Can$ 25. One should, however, check the invoice carefully *(→Accommodation).*

Youth Hostel: 193 York Street, NB E3B 3N8, Tel: (506) 454-1233, Can$ 6 for members, Can$ 9 for non-members, open from June 1 to September 1.

Motels: ''Norfolk Motel,'' NB E3B 5W5, Tel: (506) 472-3278, 20 rooms from Can$ 25, on NS-Route 2 on the outskirts of the city.

''Airport Motel,'' Box 4, Site 10, RR No. 1, NB E3B 4X2, Tel: (506) 458-9706, 21 rooms from Can$ 29, near the airport.

''Skyline Motel,'' 502 Forest Hill Road, NB E3B 4K4, Tel: (506) 455-6683, 27 rooms from Can$ 30.

''Country Motel,'' RR No. 6, NB E3B 5X7, Tel: (506) 459-3464, 6 rooms from Can$ 30.

In addition, there are about a dozen more expensive alternatives.

Airport: Fredericton Airport, Box 1 Site 15, RR No. 1, E3B 4X2. The airport is on Lincoln Road, 20 kilometres southeast of the city near Oromocto and can only be reached by taxi. The train only transports freight.

Bus Terminal: Cross-country lines SMT, 101 Regent Street, E3B 3W5, Tel: (506) 458-8350.

Buses: ''Fredericton Transit'' connects the suburbs with the city. The public regional bus lines meet at King's Place in the centre of the city. The small bus company ''Trius Service'' operates a van service from the passenger train stops, from Frederic Junction Train Station to ''Beaverbock Hotel'' in the city and back.

Information: Tourist Information Centre, City Hall, Queen Street, P.O. Box 130, Fredericton, NB E3B 4Y7, Tel: (506) 452-9500.

Train Station: VIA Rail Station Fredericton Junction, located 40 kilometres south of the city.

Fuel

There are service stations in the wilderness along every highway in such sufficient numbers that one will never find oneself in an awkward situation. However those who do not have a spare canister with them should fill the tank when it is half full.

Due to the varying tax rates in the individual provinces (Québec has the highest with 14 cents per litre) and the varying market conditions, large difference in prices develop in Canada. The price per litre in Québec is between 52 and 59 cents (depending on the octane level).

At the filling stations one will encounter five different types of fuel: ''regular'' (leaded normal), ''regular unleaded'' (unleaded normal), ''premium'' (leaded super), ''premium unleaded'' (unleaded super) and diesel.

Gaspésie

Among the beautiful examples of nature in Québec, the peninsula of Gaspé
certainly ranks highest on the list. Extending south of the St. Lawrence River,
the massive ridge of the Appalachians far to the east protrudes into the Gulf
of St. Lawrence. On the outermost point is the small town of Gaspé. The name
of the city and the peninsula comes from the Micmac language: Gaspeg is
said to mean "the land's end." South of the peninsula, the Baie des Chaleurs
extends far to the west into the country's interior. In between are mostly im-
penetrable alpine forests, mainly in the form of several provincial parks, which
are protected under conservation laws.

The peninsula can be traversed on the approximately 1,600 kilometre long
coastal road. The stretch can also be travelled by the Greyhound bus
"Voyageur." At the beginning of the peninsula, it is more heavily populated
with a series of magnificent old Seigneurien — manor houses formerly belonging to the French aristocracy in the villages located along the river — but the
landscape then quickly becomes more mountainous, more barren and more
solitary. Out in this region, life is more leisurely, original and noticeably Old
French. Small fishing villages are nestled into the mountain recesses and fjords.
From some of these, one can transport one's car by ferry to the PQ Route
138, running parallel to the north banks of the St. Lawrence River.

The outermost point of Gaspésie is a natural reserve called Forillon National
Park. Its purpose is to protect the landscape formations of coastal cliffs, fjords
and sand beaches with their variety of bird life as well as rare species of plants
among the conifer groves. The park has an excellent infrastructure and allows
for experiencing nature in every form. Five campsites are available in the park
measuring only 200 square kilometres. Ample accommodation is available in
the fishing villages on the outer edge of the peninsula as well as in the town
of Gaspé in all price categories.

Information: Superintendant Parc national Forillon, 146 Boulevard Gaspé, C.P.
1220, Gaspé PQ G0C 1R0, Tel: (418) 368-5505.

To the south of the Baie des Chaleurs are a number of beach resorts, of which,
Percé is the most widely known because of its rock formations. A wall-like island

*The dimensions of the Christ Church in Fredericton appear somewhat exag-
gerated for the small provincial capital of New Brunswick* ▶

composed of cliffs towers 100 metres above the water, extending 500 metres. During low tide, the island is surrounded only by the ocean floor. What is especially interesting about this island is the massive 17 metre gap in the rock which was carved out of the cliffs by the tides.

The attractiveness of the landscape, the scenery in the alpine wilderness and the extensive areas of water reaching to the horizon will ensure that a trip to Gaspésie will leave a lasting impression.

Gold

In Canada, gold can be found in just about every river or stream — but the amount is limited to only traces. In general, panning for gold is not worthwhile and has never been worthwhile (with few exceptions, even though one will still often come across those determined souls in search of their shimmering dream). At the end of the year, most prospectors will have earned less through their efforts than they have paid out for provisions and equipment over the course of the year. Striking it rich, therefore, happens only very rarely. What is worthwhile is the industrial extraction of gold. This, however requires a great deal of investment and heavy equipment. All of the gold in the rivers and streams originates from the eroded rock layers washed into nearby waterways. The precious metal is contained in veins or larger scattered deposits in the rock. Therefore, the point of origin of the gold in the rivers and streams is usually the object of the search. As long as the gold has not already been completely eroded from the rock and washed into the waterways, it is mined from the rock using either conventional methods or employing dynamite. Hard rock mining is what this is called as opposed to digging for placer gold, prospecting or panning for gold in stream beds.

Amateurs who would like to try their luck with a shovel and pan can do so in Canada. But caution is advised! Even claims presumed to be abandoned are taboo!

Every marked-off plot of land must first be claimed as private property. One should refrain from all prospecting activities as these can be penalised by law. The owner of the prospecting rights is usually not overly friendly in such cases and is allowed to be rigorous in excercising his right of ownership. It is best to first stick to the commercially operated ''practice'' panning businesses. Here, one is taught the techniques of panning for a small fee and is also alowed to keep any gold found. One is always successful to some degree because "pay dirt" is brought in from well-known gold mining areas.

In addition to this, there is ample literature available to inform the amateur. The prospector's "Bible" is the "Bostock Report," compiled by the geologist H.S. Bostock. "Selected Field Reports of the Geological Survey of Canada" contains a list of where gold has been discovered to date and one can thumb through this book at most libraries. Further information can be obtained through the Chamber of Mines, Box 4427, Whitehorse YT Y1A 3T5. This chamber also runs a prospector's academy. Those with enough time can take part in a course on the theory and practice of prospecting.

The gold washing pans, available everywhere as souvenirs, are authentic and are also a must for those setting out in search of self-prospected riches. These pans, however, must first be prepared for use because they are covered with a fine oil film to prevent rusting. The pan should not be washed with soap. The metal should be somewhat rough so that the gold dust remains in the pan. The best is still the oldest and simplest prospector's method: in the evening before beginning prospecting, one should completely fill the pan with hot coals and ashes from the campfire. The pan is then set into the fire when only coals and ashes remain. The next morning the pan is ready for use, although probably no longer nice enough to use back home as a soup dish or as a wall decoration. Rough, discoloured, spotted and almost rusted is the best condition for a pan when separating the glittering dust from the black sand.

Gros Morne National Park

The almost 200 square kilometre large Gros Morne National Park is located in the middle portion of the western coast of Newfoundland on the Gulf of St. Lawrence across from the mainland of Québec. It has an excellent infrastructure, the NF Route 430 transverses the park from south to north in its entire length. The unique western coast of Newfoundland is punctuated by fjords, and this landscape and geological composition is to be preserved. For this reason, this park has been added to the list of UNESCO World Heritage Sites, giving it additional protection.

The fjords protrude up to 450 metres high from the approximately 20 kilometre long Brook Pond. Large portions of the mountains belonging to the Canadian Shield are barren as they always have been. The park administration offers guided tours and in some attractive fishing villages amid the fjords, one can rent boats to tour the coast or fish. The park is available for all types of outdoor activities. An additional road in the southern portion of the park is the NF Route 431, which follows after the largest fjord "Bonne Bay." One can spend the night at the Lomond Campground, run by the park administration for Can\$ 5. Among the three additional campgrounds run by the park administration is the Berry Hill Campground, 4 kilometres north of Rocky Harbour on NF Route 430. This campground offers the most comfort and costs, therefore, Can\$ 8 per night.

The biggest attraction in the park is, in addition to the impressive coastal formations, the small caribou herds protected by wildlife preservation laws in Newfoundland.

Information: Superintendent Gros Morne National Park, Box 130, Rocky Harbour NF A0K 4N0, Tel: (709) 458-2066.

Halifax

As is the case with so many North American cities, Halifax, the capital of Nova Scotia (population: 114,594) can also accredit its existence to a harbour — the uniquely formed, natural harbour basin. Taking on the function of a breaker, McNab's island cuts across the entrance to the harbour, protecting it from the waves of the Atlantic. Further beyond is the first harbour basin — Halifax Harbour. Situated on its west bank is the city of Halifax with its harbour, downtown area and citadel. Toward the northwest, the breadth of the harbour lessens. Located here on the narrows, across the river from Halifax is the city of Dartmouth, linked with Halifax by two highway bridges, the MacDonald and the MacKay bridges; both are toll bridges. And adjacent to the narrows is Bedford Basin, an extensive harbour, the potential of which has yet to be fully realised. An additional fjord, extending from the entry to the harbour separates Halifax almost completely from the mainland so that the city seems to be situated on a peninsula surrounded by Halifax Harbour and the Northwest Arm. It is then not surprising that Halifax is the home of the Canadian Atlantic Marine Corps.

Halifax / **History**

The settlement of Halifax, in terms of historical events, is still young in origin. It was in 1749 that the British commander Colonel Cornwallis declared the harbour a docking point for the English armed forces. Construction on the fortress complex, the *Halifax Citadel,* overlooking the harbour, began immediately. It was completed in 1856 but was already superfluous even before construction began. It was never attacked in its history. In 1956, it was declared a National Historic Site and made into an outdoor museum. Today, students from Halifax, clad in historical uniforms (as Royal highlanders, naturally in the Scottish kilt) parade through the complex and on the hill, to reenact the attack on the fort which never occurred.

Halifax / **Sights**

The *Historic Properties* in the old district of the city reflect a colourful portion of the past and are by all means worth visiting. Amidst the "second largest natural harbour in the world" is a complete block of houses which has remained

The wall-like cliffs of Percé Island (Gaspésie) tower 100 metres above the water

preserved in its original condition. Surrounded by a boardwalk are the ship-builders' houses and the former warehouses of shipping companies. Today, a shopping street with original pubs is tucked behind the historical facades. On McNab's Island at the entry to the harbour, one will find old fortifications. The ferry from Cable Wharf brings visitors across the channel. Most of them find the beach and the facilities on the shore more attractive than the complexes. In the summer, festivals also take place here.

Those who by now have not yet seen enough military complexes can visit yet another fortress, *York Redouble* from the year 1793. Located here are even more historical relics. The fortress can be reached in 15 minutes from the downtown area of Halifax, taking NS Route 253 to the harbour entrance.

The landmark of Halifax is, however, the *Old Town Clock* at the base of the citadel. The clock and bell tower were brought over from London by Prince Edward in 1803. The son of King George III became the supreme commander of the country's military forces — which was not even necessary at that time. Among the parks in the capital, the *Halifax Public Garden* is especially worth mentioning. It is truly a magnificent park, which one should definitely visit. Although some moderately tall buildings lend the city a modern appearance, Halifax has maintained its unmistakable small town flair. The old core of the settlement has remained preserved and most of the important administration buildings were already built under the rule of Queen Victoria's father around 1800. The *St. Paul's Anglican Church,* the oldest Protestant building in Canada has been standing since 1759. Among the galleries in the city, the *Art Gallery of Nova Scotia* stands apart from the rest, maintaining its own high standards. It is housed in the former *Dominion Building* dating back to 1876, located at Hollis Street 1741. This historic building has had a large number of functions over the years, having served as a post office, a customs house, a courthouse and a police presidium for the Royal Canadian Mounted Police (RCMP).

In addition to no less than eight universities and institutions of higher education, the city is home to numerous theatres, museums and galleries. On rainy days, it will never prove boring to visit one of the special cultural events which take place almost daily during the summer.

Halifax / **Practical Information**

Accommodation

Bed & Breakfast: ''Boutilliers Bed & Breakfast''***, 5 Boutilliers Grove, Dart-mouth, NS B2X 2V9. Open from January to October, prices range from Can$ 40 to 45.

''Caroline's B & B,'' 134 Victoria Road, Dartmouth, NS B3A 1V6. Open all year. 3 rooms, two baths, prices from Can$ 25 and 30.

''Fresh Start Bed & Breakfast''***, 2720 Gottingen Street, Halifax, NS B3K 3C7. 5 rooms, prices from Can$ 35 to 50.

Guest House: ''Fountain View Guest House,'' 2138 Robie Street, Halifax, NS B3K 4M5. Open all year, 7 rooms, 4 baths, prices from Can$ 24 to 30.

Hotels: ''King Edward Inn,'' 5780 West Street, corner of West and Acricola Street, Halifax, NS. Open all year, 44 rooms, prices from Can$ 55 and 65.

''The Cat and Fiddle Inn,'' 1946 Oxford Street, Halifax, NS B3H 4A2. Open all year, 12 rooms, prices from Can$ 34 to 44.

''The Lord Nelson Hotel''*, 1515 South Park Street, Box 700, Halifax, NS B3J 2T3. Open all year, 210 rooms, prices from Can$ 58 to 108.

''Welcome Inn,'' 1254 Hollis Street, Halifax, NS B3J 1Z6. Open all year, 27 rooms, 13 baths, prices from Can$ 27 to 40.

Airport: Halifax International Airport, P.O. Box 470, Dartmouth, NS B2Y 2Y8, Tel: (902) 427-5500. 25 kilometres north of the city, no public transportation available to the airport. There are, however, airport buses offering shuttle ser-vices to and from the larger hotels (from 6 am to 10 pm). Those who have not booked these hotels must ensure that the driver drops them off somewhere near their hotel.

Buses: The bus terminal is located northeast of the city centre, on the corner of Robie and Almon Street. The Acadian Lines Ltd. (6040 Almon Street, Halifax, NS B3K 1T8, Tel: (902) 429-8421) operates on a long distance network serving the province of Nova Scotia. Greyhound passes are valid for these buses.

Information: Nova Scotia Tourism and Culture, 4th Floor, Cornwallis Place, 1601 Water Street, Halifax, NS B3J 3C6. Open Monday to Friday from 8:30 am to 4:30 pm.

Restaurants

"The Halifax Lobster Feast," 5078 George Street, Halifax Ferry Wharf, NS B3J 1M4. Restaurant on board the former Halifax/Dartmouth ferry; lobster, seafood, large salad bar. Open from May 15 to October 15, daily from 4 to 11 pm.

"Le Bistro Café," 1333 South Park Street, Halifax, NS B3J 2K9. Light dishes, fish, Sunday brunch. Familiar and friendly atmosphere, in summer, one can sit outside. Thursday and Sunday, classical guitar music. Open all year, daily from 11:30 am to 11:30 pm.

"Voilà Restaurant," 5140 Prince Street, NS B3J 1L4. French cuisine. Open all year, Tuesday to Friday from 11:30 am to 2:30 pm and Tuesday to Sunday from 6 to 10 pm, closed Monday.

"Satisfaction Feast Restaurant and Bakery," 1581 Grafton Street, NS B3J 2C3. Vegetarian dishes, complete dinners, whole grain bakery, children's portions. Open all year, Monday to Saturday from 11 am to 10 pm, Sunday 4 to 7 pm.

"The Halliburton House," 5184 Morris Street, NS B3J 1B3. Fish and seafood,

Protected by nature preservation laws — Forillon National Park with its rugged landscape, flora and fauna

roasted duck, homemade desserts, children's menu. Open all year, daily from 6 to 9 pm.

Train Station: VIA Rail Inc., 1161 Hollis Street, Halifax, NS B3H 2P6, Tel: (902) 429-8421. The station is located in the centre of the city, south of the harbour, on the southern portion of Hollis Street.

History

For millions of years, the North American continent was uninhabited. Neither great apes nor their cousins, the homo sapiens, had evolved here.

The first humans immigrated to the continent approximately 40,000 years ago. It is presumed that during certain times of the year a land bridge was passable between Siberia and Alaska, where the Aleutian Islands protrude from the Bering Strait. In constantly varying groups and waves of peoples, the ancestors of the present-day North American Indians came first to the continent. Their relatives who arrived earlier continued further on their exodus or wandered

An unparalleled coastline separated by fjords in the western part of New-foundland — the Gros Morne National Park

past them, thus populating the entire continent from west to east and all the way south to Tierra del Fuego. It was only relatively late in the development (5000 years ago) that the Inuit were to follow them in crossing the Bering Strait. Both groups are often referred to as "natives" on the North American continent. The ethnic groups themselves are opposed to this expression and choose to call themselves "the first people." As is presumed to be true today, and as can be supported in a few rare cases by archaeological finds like paintings and drawings, America had already been visited by Europeans crossing the Atlantic in its early stages of development. Phoenicians, Irishmen, Vikings and fishermen from Europe's western coast had reached the American continent long before Columbus. These people traded, brought back wood and fished for cod, which was in abundance off of the coast of Newfoundland. In this way the demand for fish for the numerous Christian holidays in Europe could be met.

With the rediscovery of the sea passage to the new continent by Christopher Columbus in 1492, the European colonisation began. Resulting from the Spanish captain's journey, two enterprises played a definitive role in the northern part of the continent: John Cabot travelled through the Maritimes, commissioned by the English in 1497 and 1498; Jacques Cartier did so on order of the French crown in 1534 and 1535. Both declared the eastern region of Canada national domain of their respective rulers — and both disregarded the wishes of the Indians inhabiting the region at that time. Thus, the war between the English and the French began, fought on the Atlantic coast over a period of two centuries with brief interruptions. From the year 1763, the french were surpressed. The region, which was composed of about 20 English colonies, some of which were self-governing, was unified under English rule. This changed with the Boston Tea Party of July 4 1774. The battle for independence which led to the founding of the USA was in no way applauded unanimously by the population. Even though, on the one hand, the Catholic conviction of the French-speaking majority in the Maritimes and Quebec proved to have a dampening effect, the veritable exodus of Royalists and Loyalists commenced. Some immigrated for personal reasons and some due to the express endorsement of the Republican party; the result was over a hundred thousand people flooding northwards. The English monarchy supported this exodus by offering financial compensation and integration support.

This development lead to a more dense settlement of the Maritimes, the statistical outflanking of the French-speaking population, and thus, the marked linguistic conflict still in existence. This brought on the development of the predominantly English-speaking province of Upper Canada (now Ontario) and the stabilisation of a consistently US-hostile structure of the population. When the United States attacked the remaining English colonies in 1812, hoping to incorporate these into the US, they ran into the embittered resistance of the Canadians. The USA lost the two-year war, and could consider themselves lucky that the previous status quo was guaranteed to them in the peace treaty of 1814.

On the other hand, the Republican neighbours did not remain without intellectual influence on the way Canadians perceived themselves. During this time, the distinction was made between Upper Canada, Lower Canada and the Maritimes. To outline roughly, Upper Canada included the settled areas of what is now Ontario along the Great Lakes, Lower Canada encompassed present-day Québec along the lower valley of the St. Lawrence River. In addition, there were the four Maritime provinces. Serious uprisings and local rebellion which lead to injuries and deaths spurred Queen Victoria to action. She united both Canadas in 1841 and granted the colony self-government, giving it the right to form its own parliament. The first capital was Kingston, Ontario until 1857 when it became Ottawa. On July 1, 1867, the Queen enacted the "North America Act" with which the Maritimes were added to the Canadian Union at their own request (Prince Edward Island delayed joining the union a few years, however, entering the union in 1873). In 1870, the Province on the opposite side of the continent, British Columbia, joined the union. In the course of the same year, the Canadian government bought the rights to sovereignty for the country's interior, which were held by the Hudson's Bay Company up until this time. These regions became the Canadian provinces of Manitoba, Saskatchewan and Alberta as well as the two Territories. Newfoundland was the twelfth and last province to join the Canadian union in 1949.

Canada is a federalistic nation. The head of state is the English crown represented by a royally appointed governor general. The Canadian government under the prime minister answers to the parliament which, in accordance with the English model, has an upper and lower house.

The twelve provinces each have their own parliament, the legislative branch. The minister president of each province is responsible to the one-chamber provincial parliament. In addition, the ten fully autonomous federal states have a lieutenant governor, a delegate of the English crown. This is, however, not the case for the two territories which fall under the authority of the federation in Ottawa: due to their sparse population (25,000 and 50,000 residents respectively) they are not capable of levying enough taxes to cover their expenditures.

Holidays and Celebrations

Holidays in all of Canada and additional holidays in each province or territory almost all fall conveniently on Monday. Even the holidays for the saints follow this rule; thus, they fall on a different day each year. This makes it difficult to give the exact dates. This is important for visitors to know because neither the banks nor the ministries are open on these days.

Also, all of the larger stores, museums and some of the restaurants follow suit. This is not true of the smaller stores and the grocery stores which are always open. The tourist must also count on many Canadians being on the roads, filling the restaurants and recreation parks.

Holidays

New Year's Day: January 1

Good Friday

St. Patrick's Day: the Monday nearest to March 17

Easter Monday

St. George's Day: the Monday nearest to April 23

Victoria Day: Queen Victoria's Birthday, May 24, 1819; the Monday after the second to last Sunday in May

Discovery Day: the Monday nearest to June 24

Canada Day: national holiday; July 1

Memorial Day: the Monday nearest to July 1

Orangeman's Day: the Monday nearest to July 12

Labour Day: the first Monday in September

Thanksgiving Day: the second Monday in October

Remembrance Day: November 11

Christmas Day: December 25

Despite a moderate number of high-rises — Halifax has remained a small, unpretenious town ▶

Boxing Day: December 26 (not in the Province of Québec!)
Furthermore, each province celebrates its own additional holidays.
Celebrations and special events →*individual town entries*

Hudson's Bay Company

During the mid 17th century, the French settlers and traders had soon
discovered the abundance and profitability of the fur trade in northern Canada
and along the St. Lawrence River for the European market. Important market
places developed from two Indian settlements on the river; today, these are
called Québec and Montréal. French governors practised protectionism over
the French fur monopoly, which brought the crown more than adequate compensation for the lack of gold for which he had hoped. The fur trade brought
similar wealth into the coffers of France as gold had done for Spain.

Among the new adventurers wanting to quickly acquire a fortune were Medard
Chouart, Sieur des Groseilliers and his son-in-law Pierre Esprit Radisson.
Through their good relationship to the Indians and even to the land itself, they
were very successful. This did not bring them the desired riches, but rather
the envy of the governor. He, who was only a minor monarch far away from
the supervision of his king, quickly found an excuse to confiscate the fur
shipments. The riches were thus diverted to a completely different pocket.
This ploy proved to be unwise. The governor was able to rely on his no less
corrupt and well-bribed counterparts at the court of Versailles, but not on the
resigned acceptance of the victims he defrauded. When their complaint was
quickly dismissed at the court of Versailles, the trappers travelled to England.
There, after some initial hesitation, they found the interest of King Charles II.
They received two ships and were now expected to prove that the alleged wealth
of furs were indeed present in Canada. Although the ''Eaglet'' was forced to
return because of a storm at sea, the two Frenchmen aboard the ''Nonsuch''
were successful in their journey. They sailed around the regions occupied by
France with the help of the crew and into the bay named after the English
seafarer Henry Hudson which he had discovered in 1610. They laid anchor
in the southernmost part of the bay on September 29, 1668 and built a fort
on the mouth of the big river which was first named ''Fort Charles'' after the
English king but is now called ''Fort Rupert.''

The homecoming of the "Nonsuch," packed up to the planks with furs, exceeded all expectations. Prince Rupert of Palatine, who lived in the English palace had gathered some wealthy noblemen who were willing to finance further expeditions in no time. The prince was not just any courtier; he had accomplished valuable services and brought success in a number of cases for his cousin King Charles II as well as the Admiral of the fleet, the leader of the armed forces. The king was aware of his indebtedness; and when he learned in what an inexpensive way these furs could be obtained, he was immediately willing to give Prince Rupert a pompous document. This extremely generous document presented Prince Rupert with all the land that he did not already own: almost the entire area of present-day Canada! On May 2 1670, the king signed a document in which he granted his cousin and his 17 partners "The Governor and Company of Adventurers of England, trading into Hudson's Bay" rights to ownership and sovereignty over all of the land which lay on the banks of those rivers which flow into the Hudson Bay. The residents of these areas were not consulted. Most definitely none of those involved in this development could fathom what a huge area was given away with the stroke of a pen.

With this, the cornerstone was laid for the military confrontation with France. It was not exactly a war in the conventional sense — the area was far too large and the number of Europeans, still too limited. However, when the enemies came upon one another, the result was duelling and death; both sides soon won the support of "their" Indians. This was the time in which Cooper's "The Deerslayer" takes place: thousands of harmless settlers, women and children were massacred over a hundred years during occasional attacks. The victors would destroy the settlements and forts and add the furs of the defeated to their booty.

It was only when France temporarily ended their conflict with England in the treaty of Utrecht in 1713 that the HBC could expand unhindered. Trading posts were established at a quick pace along the coast of the Hudson Bay and on the banks of the rivers leading into Canada's interior. Their "forts," actually only blockhouses, that were surrounded by a wooden palisade, became the centres for founders and settlers much later in the development of the Canadian cities. Initially, the settlers were unwelcome, they only hindered the trapping trade.

With the treaty of Paris in 1763, the monopoly of the HBC seemed to become perfect. France gave up its colonies in the northern part of the American continent and the HBC could take over these areas. But it was exactly this development that gave rise to a new competitor. English, predominantly Scottish merchants, flowed into the country giving the HBC some competition as independent merchants. When they ran into the embittered opposition of the HBC monopoly, a new conflict was to begin. In its aftermath, the newcomers banded together. The "North West Company," based in Montréal, grew rapidly into a powerful organisation.

Only now would the commercial shipping on the Canadian river system flourish, made possible by fur trading. The high time of the Voyageure, also called "Coureur du Bois," began. Without them, the two trading companies would have never succeeded in penetrating the country's interior. The woodsmen (usually of French descent), were most often the children of Indian women and French immigrants. The had the necessary skills to transport the goods into the most remote wilderness and, in late autumn, to return with the furs they received in trade. With the spring thaw, entire flotillas set off in birch bark canoes, heavily laden with goods.

The gentlemen in the two trading companies, however, were English businessmen and shareholders. Gradually, it became clear to them that the portion of their profits used to finance the perpetual conflict between the two companies ate up their returns. The time finally came in 1821: the two companies merged; the NWC was absorbed by the HBC. The period of armed conflict had come to an end, but with the new era, free trade was also introduced to Canada.

The HBC, founded in 1670, endured the free competition and is still in existence today. In all of the larger cities, one will find the company's lavish shopping centres; in every village on the edge of the populated regions of Northern Canada, one finds the HBC trading stores. Trade with all types of goods, however, is no longer the basis of the company. It has long since taken advantage of the much higher returns of holdings in mining and industrial companies.

Hunting

Foreign citizens in Canada are allowed to hunt without any problems. Licences and documents from other countries (Europe, for instance) have no significance and are not required. It is just as uncomplicated to bring firearms for hunting into the country for personal use *(→Customs Regulations).* Many provinces, however, make the use of firearms by citizens of foreign countries dependent on proof that he or she is permitted to carry that type of weapon. Therefore, as a general rule:

A notarised copy of firearms permits or the weapon or hunting licence should be brought along. Those who are not able to do this must demonstrate that they are able to handle a weapon to an official in the specific province.

Everyone who has bought a hunting licence beforehand is allowed to hunt wild game. These can be purchased at the official administrative bureaus for hunting and also at every rifle dealer and sporting goods store. The licence is valid for one year and is issued under the name of the holder. The licence must be carried when hunting.

In Canada, there are the usual seasons in which hunting is prohibited. The types of wild game that may be hunted during a specific season vary depen-

They track down the discared left-overs in the national parks — the bears

ding on the province or territory. The appropriate information on these regulations is provided free of charge upon purchase of a hunting licence.

The fees for small game hunting differ greatly as well.

Big game hunting is only possible when accompanied by an authorised hunting guide. These regulations are also different in each region. Most often, a certain region will be allocated to an experienced and certified hunting guide, in which they have the exclusive permission to lead foreign visitors on the hunt for big game. Regardless of this, every resident in Canada is allowed to hunt in the same area without a hunting guide as he or she pleases.

Identification →*Travel Documents*

Indians

''The Indians'' — both of these words are incorrect. ''The'' Indians do not exist and never have. The first settlers to journey to the American continent were not a homogeneous group. As they differ drastically in their cultures, their anatomy and appearance as well as their languages, it is assumed that a number of very different races from Asia and Siberia emigrated to America in a number of waves.

Which race descended from the first immigrants, referred to as ''Paleo-Indians,'' is no longer ascertainable. It can be concluded from the difference in appearance among their descendants that with every new wave of immigrants, new ethnic groups of people arrived, assimilated or did not assimilate, then drifted apart. Proud, tall warriors with honed Roman features are also among these groups, but in the north, only scattered. The Indian population in the north have predominantly broad, even faces and a stocky build. Those who think that these races must be close relatives of the Inuit, only are correct in regard to outward appearances. ''The'' Indians are by no means related to Mongolian races; the typical Mongolian fold of the eyelid is missing completely. Therefore, it is more probable that these Indians descended from races that lived between Mongolia and Caucasus at one time before migrating to the American continent. In terms of build and appearance, they show similarities to both races, but are most similar to Caucasians. The Indians are by no means ''redskins''! It is theorised that the Beothuk (one of the white Indian races living in Newfoundland, which was already eradicated in the 19th century) was the origination of this term. Old chronicles reported they had the custom of covering their skin with red paint from head to toe. They then wore animal pelts when the weather became colder.

If the words "the," "Indians" and "redskins" are all inappropriate, who are these people then? The easiest possible answer at present is: they were the original native Americans to first immigrate to the American continent. All have a light to dark brown skin colour, are related to the two races mentioned above, but are not identical to one another and have an unbelievable number of different and expressive languages.

In total, there are six basic linguistic families, which include about 125 distinct languages. In Eastern Canada, only two of these linguistic families are represented: Algonkin and Irokee. These do not, however, stand for certain tribes (with the exception of the small Irokee group) but merely link related linguistic systems.

Today, only Micmac Indians still live in New Brunswick, in the southern part of Newfoundland, in Nova Scotia, Québec and on Prince Edward Island; Huron Indians live in Québec as well.

Information →*Tourist Information*

Inuit

The last of the earliest immigrants to enter Canada, the Inuit, settled in the tundra in the extreme northern portion of Canada in the coastal areas and on the islands in the polar sea. The frequently used expression "Eskimo" is not well liked by the Innus. The word comes from the Indians from the linguistic family of the Athabaska and means "raw meat-eaters." To an Inuit ear this is more an insult.

The migration of the Inuit, who descended from the Mongolians, first began over 5000 years ago; the population of today in the north came even later to Canada — only 1000 years ago. Due to the remote locations of their settlements, far more of their original lifestyle and customs have endured in comparison with the Indians of the southern regions. Hunting and fishing have remained the basis of their livelihood. In addition, however, their craftsmanship gave rise to a new local industry. All over the world, one can find art dealers offering Inuit art: sculptures, lithographs and weavings.

Of the regions covered in this book, the Inuit live only on the northern coast of Labrador and in Québec. The islands in the James Bay, the main area settled by the Inuit, are a part of the Northwest Territory, as are all of the other Nordic islands.

James Bay Project

In the northern part of Québec, the polar sea protrudes far into the Canadian land mass with its southernmost arm and forms the continuation of the Hudson Bay: the James Bay. It is an extensive basin into which several large rivers flow from the entire northern slopes of the Canadian Shield, emtying the spring run-off into the basin.

Now, nature is no longer to be experienced but capitalistically exploited by the technicians. Thus the politicians, financiers and technicians agreed upon the megalomaniacal James Bay Project. In 1971, the legislation of Québec laid the legal foundation and the construction began. A 725 kilometre long roadway in the north was built, dams constructed, watershed divides broken through and rivers dammed up or diverted. Around the year 2000, it is supposed to be completed: a region a large as entire European countries will be submerged. Over 12,000 megawatts of electricity is to be produced. In addition, the use of the other rivers is also being planned.

The partially completed project which can be viewed today is a repulsive sight. In contrast to similar projects in other countries, the areas were not deforested but "drowned." For kilometres, the dying forests protrude from the rising waters. Trunks of dead trees densely line the shores; no canoes can paddle ashore. The fish in the waters are contaminated and killed off by the tanic acid, a substance contained in high quantities in the tree bark. The ramifications for the environment and the extent of the ecological damage is not foreseeable. Those who hope for the development of the north for tourism or outdoor recreation will be disappointed once more: the Province of Québec legally dictates that every visitor north of the 52nd degree of latitude must be accompanied by an officially authorised guide — of course subject to qualified reimbursement! This is not only true for canoeists and fishermen but also for those hikers who would like to pitch their tents in this area! There is no area in the northern portion of Québec where a canoe tour independently organised and at one's own risk is possible. For the payment of a guide, one must calculate Can$ 100 per day into expenses.

Kouchibouguac National Park

Measuring 238 square kilometres, the Kouchibouguac Natural Reserve Park is the largest in the province of New Brunswick and is located on its dune-covered eastern coast on the Gulf of St. Lawrence. It encompasses coastal forests and salt marshes, lagoons and narrow tongues of land, long sand beaches and tall sand dunes. A network of hiking trails covers the interior of the park, and on the coast all types of water sports are avidly pursued. The NB Route 117 runs through the park from south to north and a number of roads branch off from it forming a network throughout the park's landscape.

Three simple campsites run by the park administration are available. Ample accommodation is available in the beach resort areas on the southern edge of the park and in the towns of this region.

Information: Kouchibouguac National Park, Kouchibouguac NB E0A 2A0, Tel: (506) 876-3973.

The colourful activity of the Hot Air Balloon Festival in Montréal

Labrador

The northeast corner of the continent, the Labrador region, located somewhat further north than the island of Newfoundland, has officially belonged to the Province of Newfoundland since 1927. Geologically speaking, these two mountainous regions have nothing in common. Labrador is a part of the Canadian Shield. Its peaks reach an altitude of twice that of the mountains on the island. The highest summit with the name ''Cirque Mountain'' can be found far up north near Ramah and towers 1,676 metres above sea level. Labrador has a population of about 40,000. The natives live almost exclusively in small villages in the coastal fjords and the residents are mostly Inuit. Only in the ''iron belt'' between the towns of Labradorville, NF and Sheffervill, PQ (both connected to each other by the QNSLR railroad) and in Goose Bay is the population dominated by descendants of Northern Europeans.

The only road running from Goose Bay over the 480 kilometres of gravel roadway to Esker was built in connection with the power plant project on the Churchill River. The road leads through complete seclusion along the electrical power generators. **Goose Bay** and the Hamilton Inlet is the gateway to the country. The small town of 8,000, was established as an airport base by the Allied Forces during the Second World War. It still serves as an NATO air base today and is constantly used by pilots for practice flights. More important, however, is its significance as a junction point for transportation and a centre for provisions in Labrador. Those who set out for Esker should consider that there are 295 kilometres between Goose Bay and **Churchill Falls,** the next opportunity to buy provisions, but offering no accommodation. Accommodation can be found after another 85 kilometres: ''Lobstick Lodge & Motel,'' P.O. Box 86, Churchill Falls, Labrador A0R 1A0, Tel: (709) 925-3235, 10 rooms, from Can$ 40, restaurant, outfitter/hunting guide. Open only from June 1 to October 31.

The street with the proud name ''Trans-Labrador Highway,'' ends 100 kilometres farther west in Esker, the train terminal. Here there is no accommodation. It is possible to load one's car onto the train. About 100 kilometres south, in **Ross Bay Junction,** one has access to the roadway network which leads here from Québec. In this corner of Labrador are the two mining towns of **Wabush** and **Labrador City** with a total population of 15,000 and all the necessary services.

Accommodation

Hotels: ''Sir Wilfred Grenfell Hotel,'' P.O. Box 700, Wabush, Labrador A0R 1B0, Tel: (709) 282-3221, 60 rooms, from Can$ 66, restaurant, bar.

''Two Seasons Inn,'' P.O. Box 572, Labrador City, Labrador A2V 2B6, 21 rooms, from Can$ 69, restaurant, bar.

''Carol Lodge,'' 215 Drake Avenue, Labrador City, Labrador A2V 2B6, Tel: (709) 944-7736, 23 self-maintenance apartments, from Can$ 59.

On the northern outskirts of Labrador City, 10 kilometres from the city centre is the Duley Lake Provincial Park Campground with 100 places and sand beach on the lake. In the northwest of the Island of Newfoundland, the 30-kilometre ''Strait of Belle Isle'' separates the two pieces of land. On the other side in Labrador, the NF Route 510 connects **Blanc Sablon** over a stretch of about 70 kilometres with the coastal towns all the way to Red Bay. This in turn is serviced by the coastal ferry as the southernmost docking point. This ferry (only for passengers and freight) departs regularly for the larger towns along the coast up to Nain. The rest of the smaller towns and the Inuit settlements north of Nain can only be reached by light aircraft or by a privately hired boat. In addition, the interior of Labrador is not easily accessible. ''the land that God gave to Cain'' is reserved for light aircraft transportation. On the shores of the best lakes for fishing, outfitter camps have been set up, the guides leading their guests on caribou and big-game hunts. Starting points are Goose Bay and the mining towns. A listing of the numerous guides is available from the Department of Tourism.

Canoeists must be told at this point that the rivers of Labrador and New-foundland as well, are less attractive for this sport. Both regions are mesas that then fall steeply to the ocean. All noteworthy rivers are therefore impassi-ble in large sections without exception and in no way offer holiday relaxation. For canoeing only a few sections come into question, and these are not the worth the expenses involved in reaching them by small aircraft.

On the other hand, the extensive lakes of both regions are perfect for week-long excursions by canoe. Those who cherish natural seclusion and quiet wilderness, will find what they are looking for in these regions. One must however wait and see how the situation in the areas surrounding the new Lobstick Lake/Michikamau Lake develops. The newly created lake could become *the* holiday tip. In the coastal towns of Labrador, only the following accommodation is available:

"Northern Lights Inn," L'Anse-Au-Clair, Labrador A0K 3K0, Tel: (709) 931-2332, 34 rooms, from Can$ 45, restaurant.

"Barney's Hospitality," L'Anse-Au-Loup, Labrador A0K 3L0, Tel: (709) 927-5634, 3 rooms, from Can$ 23.

"Pinware River Provincial Park Campground," 40 km north of Blanc Sablon, on NF Route 510, 25 places with good salmon and trout fishing.

"Charlottetown Inn," Charlottetown, Labrador A0K 5Y0, Tel: (709)949-4627, 7 rooms, from Can$ 40, restaurant.

"Atsanik Lodge," P.O. Box 10, Nain Labrador A0P 1L0, Tel: (709) 922-2910, 9 rooms, from Can$ 60, restaurant and bar.

The two main festivities in Labrador: "Heritage Week" takes place during the first week of February in the Labrador City Arts & Culture Centre. This is a presentation of the old and new art forms of Labrador. The "Wabush Folk Festival" during the first weekend in July is a folk festival in which local artists and artists from elsewhere take part offering musical performances.

L'Anse aux Meadows

The L'Anse aux Meadows National Historic Park is the oldest known settlement of European immigrants. It is located high in the northernmost point of Newfoundland at the end of NF Route 436 which branches off from the NF Route 430 heading north. Led only by his instincts and obscure clues in the old saga of Edda, The Norwegian Helge Ingstad began excavations here on the former Viking settlement in 1960. This settlement was founded around 1000 A.D. on a meadow sloping down to the ocean. The historically authentic ruins prove that Norsemen or Vikings lived here. However, whether this was the village in which Leif Erikson, Karlsefni or the bloody Freydis carried out the deeds described in the Edda will never be known definitely.

The excavated ruins have been roofed over and can be toured. In the museum, artifacts from the excavations can be viewed.

Those who have driven up the NF Routes 430 and 436 will have no other alternative but to return the same way. The ferries to Labrador do not transport automobiles.

L'Anse aux Meadows / **Practical Information**
Accommodation

Campsite: "Pistolet Bay," 6 km from Raleigh on the NF Route 437, 27 places, simple and free of charge.

Hotels/Motels: "Viking Motel," P.O. Box 552, Pistolet Bay, St. Anthony, NF A0K 4S0, Tel: (709) 454-3541, 11 rooms at Can$ 38, restaurant and bar.

"St. Anthony Motel," P.O. Box 187, St. Anthony, NF A0K 4S0, Tel: (709) 454-3200, 22 rooms from Can$ 45, restaurant and bar.

"Vinland Motel," P.O. Box 400, St. Anthony, NF A0K 4S0, Tel: (709) 454-8843, 31 rooms from Can$ 50, restaurant and bar.

"Howell's Tourist Home," 76 b East Street, St. Anthony, NF A0K 4J0, Tel: (709) 454-3402, 5 rooms from Can$ 21.

"Valhalla Lodge," P.O. Box 596, St. Anthony, NF A0K 4S0, Tel: (709) 623-2018, 7 rooms from Can$ 35, including a hearty "Newfie" breakfast (fish and brewies).

Information: Superintendent L'Anse aux Meadows National Historic Park, P.O. Box 70, St. Lunaire-Griquet, NF A0K 2X0, Tel: (709) 623-2601.

The Gros Morne National Park was added to the list of World Heritage Sites by the UNESCO

The Laurentian Mountains

Canada's mountainous region north of the St. Lawrence River is dominated by the oldest mountain range in the world which appears under different names in different books. One of these names, ''The Pre-Cambrian Shield'' is derived from the fact that this range emerged during the Pre-Cambrian era, over 260 million years ago.. Other names for these mountains are ''Canadian Shield,'' and ''Laurentia.''

These all refer to the mountain range dominating the east of Canada and bordered to the south by the St. Lawrence River Basin. In a sweeping half-circle from the St. Lawrence River, the mountain ranges surround the broad depression in the northern region of the Northwest Territories. Today this sub-alpine wilderness of stone is completely unproductive. Only forests grow here. Even in the valleys, the topsoil is insufficient to support other botanical life. The Pre-Cambrian Shield protrudes jaggedly from the ocean, or the St. Lawrence River valley in the north of the Province of Québec, in Labrador and in Newfoundland. It is an uninterrupted mountain and forest wilderness reaching altitudes over 1000 metres above sea level. Its landscape gradually changes to tundra, and many times only bare rock is visible.

Laurentide Parks

Extending north of the cities of Ottawa, Montréal and Québec is a series of provincial parks encompassing the broad area of the Laurentide plateau. This is subdivided into a dozen independent partitions each with their own park administration. The purpose of these parks is to protect and preserve the large wilderness areas of mountain forest, but predominantly, the Laurentides serve as recreation for the residents of the cities and are equipped with roads and hiking paths. In winter they provide winter sports facilities including restaurants, ski slopes, ski lifts and accommodation. The largest of these parks, La Réserve Faunique La Vérendrye with its formidable size of 13,615 square kilometres (making it the second largest park in the province of Quebec) is interspersed with a network of interconnected lakes. These provide more than 1000 kilometres of waterways for canoeists. Unfortunately, not always the best conditions exist since the water level is maintained artificially. Depending on water demand, the shores can become unsightly areas of swampland. In addition, some of the forests were flooded instead of clearing out the reservoir basin beforehand. Decaying trunks and branches along the swamp-like banks are, therefore, not rare.

Information: Association touristique de Laurentides, 14142, rue de Lachapelle, R.R. no. 1, Saint-Jérôme (Québec), Tel: (514) 834-2535.

Madeleine Islands

The twelve islands in the archipelagos Iles de la Madeleine are located one hundred kilometres north of Prince Edward Island in the Gulf of St. Lawrence. Only seven of these islands are inhabited. The Madeleine Islands and Prince Edward Island have their geological structure and sandstone composition in common. However, they belong to the province of Québec. Six of the islands are joined by narrow strips of land which encircle some lagoons. The PQ Route 199 links eight towns on six islands, making up 85 kilometres of roadways in the form of a circuit. In addition, country roads encompass all of the larger islands. Ile d'Entrée is reachable only by ferry. All of the islands are composed of sandstone cliffs which reach a height of up to 100 metres above sea level in the interior of the islands. These cliffs are often surrounded by extensive sand dunes and lagoons. A total of 300 kilometres of sand beaches await the avid swimmer.

Madeleine Islands / **History**

Jacques Cartier had reported his discovery of the uninhabited islands and Champlain included them in his map of the region, naming them ''La Madeleine.'' The settlement of these islands first began with the persecution of the Acadians in 1755; they fled to these islands to escape the oppression. In 1787, according to the customs of that time, a wealthy nobleman was given the islands as a fief. He took advantage of this gift and mercilessly exploited the islands' residents. They consequently fled this serfdom in several waves, establishing a number of settlements on the mainland: Blanc Sablon, Sept-Iles and Havre Saint-Pierre came into being in this way. It was in 1895 that a provincial act of Québec freed the islands' residents, putting an end to the serfdom. Today, approximately 9,000 people live on the islands. These are main-ly Franco-Canadians, the descendants of the Acadians

Madeleine Islands / **Economy**

Originally, fishing was the economic basis on the islands. Later, hunting seals in winter was added as a source of income. Today, tourism is a requisite for the islands' financial survival. The touristic infrastructure is well developed. There is, however, no hustle and bustle on the islands. Those who come here will profit from the healthy Atlantic climate and enjoy the solitude of the beaches. Facilities and equipment are also available for every type of water sport. Two car rental agencies offer vehicles for touring the islands. Because discovering the countryside by bicycle is much more relaxing, one can, of course, also rent a bicycle. In addition, it is recommended to enjoy the culinary specialties of the two dozen restaurants where fine seafood cuisine is emphasised. The only ''industry'' on the islands, a salt quarry, will be found only by those who deliberately look for it.

The Province of Québec offers excellent conditions for winter sports

Madeleine Islands / **Practical Information**

Accommodation: 5 campsites, all quite comfortably equipped with shower and WC, washing machines and dryers are available, places from Can$ 5. 14 hotels/motels offer rooms from Can$ 25 to Can$ 100 per night.

Information: Association touristique des Iles-de-la-Madeleine, C.P. 1028, Cap-aux-Meules, Ile-de-la-Madeleine, PQ G0B 1B0, Tel: (418) 986-2245.

Travelling to the islands: The airport of this archipelagos is located on the centre island, Ile-du-Havre-aux-Maisons, and has daily connections to the two large cities of Montréal and Halifax. Additional flights also leave for the Gaspé peninsula (Gaspé City and Mont-Joli).

Ferry connections (car and passenger) operate between Souri, Prince Edward Island and Cap-aux-Meules. In the summer, a ferry departs daily; the trip lasts about 5 hours. A passenger boat for 15 people and freight (no cars) departs weekly for Cap-aux-Meules from Montréal.

Maps

Maps of Canada can be purchased or ordered in most bookstores. These are usually the most popular Rand McNally maps which are excellently suited for travel by car and also include information for cross-country trips. These are available as single maps but also as booklets and as an atlas.

Official topographical maps are more difficult to come by, but when planning to hike in a certain region, one will find such a map essential.

For canoeists planning trips on the rivers, these are indispensable because only they show the rapids and waterfalls. In Canada these maps are scaled 1:50,000. There are several thousand of these maps that cover the northern part of the continent! Not all corners of the continent are covered, they are not always precise, but they serve their purpose. The next scale sizes for maps are 1:250,000 and 1:500,000, but these are only useful for hikers and canoeists to convey a general picture. For metropolitan areas and heavily populated regions, there are other detailed maps but not for the wilderness. The only exception: for national parks, there are separate maps varying in scale covering a given park. These can be purchased at the park entrances (ranger stations) and from the appropriate ministries. However, none of these maps can substitute the topographically detailed maps.

In most countries these maps are difficult to come by; a bookstore will usually only be able to order them from Canada directly, saving the customer the effort if not the time. Regardless if a bookstore or the customer orders the maps from Canada directly, it can take a very long time — in Europe allow up to three months.

Those who wish to purchase these maps directly from the officials in Canada will pay at least Can$ 4 per map. First be sure to order the index of maps available (free of charge). This will include a price list and order form. This index is absolutely necessary because only with this index is it possible to find the appropriate map and its proper name and order number.

When the order form is complete, one then adds the prices according to the price list and includes this sum as advance payment plus postage and handling charges (in Europe, this is usually Can$ 5).

One can include a cheque in Canadian dollars as payment. Those in Europe should be aware, however, that such a cheque will take up to six weeks to clear, and the order will not be processed until it has. With smaller sums, one can include payment in cash; this will speed up the processing.

Address: Canada Map Office, 615 Booth Street, Ottawa Ontario K1A 0E9.

The least expensive option in buying maps is to buy them in Canada locally at bookstores or sporting goods stores. If just that one map that one happens to need is sold out, then contact the official information offices in the provincial capitals. One will be able to purchase the appropriate maps — at the best price.

Maritimes

Maritimes is the collective term for Canada's Atlantic provinces. Originally, these were only New Brunswick, Nova Scotia and Prince Edward Island. In 1949 by a supplementary referendum, the previously independent English colony of Newfoundland joined the Canadian Union. Since then, all four of these are classified as the ''sea provinces.''

Medical Care

Medical care in Canada is well organised and of excellent quality. The costs for this type of medical care are appropriately high as well. Per day, in-patient hospital treatment costs about £ 350 (US$ 570). In addition, in some provinces foreign citizens must pay an extra fee.

No emergency treatment is ever denied due to inadequate funds, but payment must then be arranged later.

Therefore, it is well-advised to ask one's health insurance company whether all medical care expenses incurred in Canada will be fully reimbursed, and what the reimbursement procedure is.

It might be a good idea to take out a supplemental travel health insurance policy which will provide the necessary supplemental coverage at a minimum of cost.

Addresses and telephone numbers of physicians are available at the visitor's centres in the major cities.

Modes of Payment

One should bring only dollars when travelling to Canada. One will have difficulties exchanging many European currencies.

Eurocheques and other cheques can also be left at home. The European cheque system is not accepted in Canada. Taking large sums of cash is also not a good idea, therefore, the best option is to buy traveller's cheques. One can buy these at any bank or other financial institutions in the denominations required. One can use traveller's cheques like cash or one can cash a traveller's cheque at a bank. One should buy one of the two types of traveller's cheques which are accepted everywhere as cash: American Express or Thomas Cook. They are insured against loss or theft and are immediately refunded in these cases.

Also recommended is a internationally recognised credit card. Mastercard/Eurocard and Visa are the most widely accepted in Canada. Other cards are accepted only at hotels or large department stores.

→*Currency*

Money →*Currency, Modes of Payment*

Montréal

Montréal, located in the Province of Québec on the St. Lawrence River, has a population of over a million. It might possibly be the city in which one comes

closest to Canada, being a true cross-section of Canada with its many nationalities, cultures and customs.

The vibrant city of Montréal with its many high rise buildings is on an island
in a tributary of the Ottawa River. Laval, also an island, is separated from the
mainland by another tributary of the Rivière des Outaouais. The Ottawa River
flows into the St. Lawrence River southwest of the city. Together, these form
the broad Lac des Deux Montages. From here, a similarly broad tributary flows
to the northeast branching into two rivers. The Rivière des Mille Isles, the "river
of a thousand islands" (which is almost correct), separates the two islands
from the mainland. The other arm is called Rivière des Prairies, which divides
the two islands from each other. North of the metropolis, the rivers reunite,
flowing into the St. Lawrence River.

Montréal / **History**

The location was the aspect of Montréal which made Jacques Cartier stop
and ponder upon laying anchor there in 1635. He quickly recognised that he
was not — as he had hoped — on his way to China. The rapids removed any
doubt as to the river character of the supposed strait.

He laid anchor near the Indians, who lived here in their large village of
Hochelaga. He dubbed a massive hill rising above the river at the centre of
the Montréal — "Mont Royal." The rapids which put an end to his journey
are still called "Lachine," because he had suspected to find China behind them.
The channelled St. Lawrence seaway allows deep-sea vessels to pass upstream and through the Great Lakes to Duluth (located on the edge of Lake
Superior) and Chicago (on the banks of Lake Michigan). China, however, still
cannot be reached via this passage.

The first settlement was established in 1642, built at the end of the sea route
to Europe used at that time. The pious Paul de Chomedey, Sieur de Maisonneuve and his accompanying abbess Jeanne Mance brought 40 settlers along;
however, they were more interested in converting the heathens. They named
their settlement "Ville-Marie." A fur trading post quickly developed from the
mission located on what was later to be called Place Royal. Even then, the
conditions for transportation contributed to a rapid boom. From this point, the
fur trading trails led into Canada's interior and the harbour served the shipping of the furs. For over two hundred years, the Ottawa River was the main

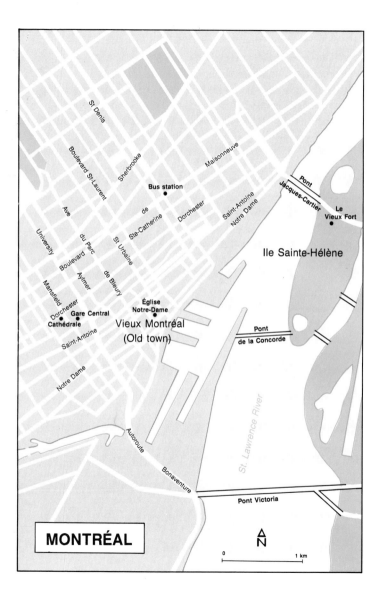

St. Denis

Boulevard St-Laurent

Sherbrooke

Maisonneuve

Bus station

Ave

de

Ste-Catherine

Dorchester

Saint-Antoine
Notre Dame

Pont
Jacques-Cartier

Le
Vieux Fort

University

du Parc

St. Urbaine

Île Sainte-Hélène

Boulevard

Aylmer

de Bleury

Mansfield

Dorchester

Église
Notre-Dame

Cathédrale

Gare Central

Vieux Montréal
(Old town)

Pont
de la Concorde

Saint-Antoine

Notre Dame

St. Lawrence River

Autoroute

Bonaventure

Pont Victoria

MONTRÉAL

N

0   1 km

artery for transporting goods into the country's interior and furs to the city. From Montréal, Canada's west up to the Rocky Mountains and northwards to the polar sea was explored, developed, and its natural resources, exploited. Traders founded the North West Company here, which soon became the large competition of the (also British) Hudson's Bay Company. Explorers from both companies developed the river systems and trade routes, and there were also conflicts over the furs trapped by the Indians — sometimes with high prices, sometimes with bloody battles. In 1821, the problem was solved in good capitalistic manner. Both companies joined forces, and thus, overcame the annoying competition. Before this, the aspiring city surrendered to the British troops under General Amherst around the old squares in Vieux Montréal, Place Royale, Place d'Youville and Place d'Armes on September 8, 1760. Under English rule, the British traders (predominantly from Scotland) now entered the market with their capital. Montréal grew and grew. The new traffic routes for railroads and later for the automobile all converged at the harbour. Trade and industry had found a choice location. Immigrants and migrants soon found work and were assimilated into the general population. The city was splitting at the seams. The old walls were razed without being replaced, the sea of buildings in the city reached almost to the banks and across the river into new suburbs. Finally, Montréal grew into a North American style city, a forest of skyscrapers, a Manhattan on the St. Lawrence River with a surprising and impressive big city panorama.

Luckily, the old city core remained intact while the construction boom in neighbouring areas has continued relentlessly, recently spurred on by the Expo 67, the 1976 Olympic Games, and the botanical exhibition in 1980. This is a reason for the unparalleled subway network which is linked to the perfect enhancement of the above-ground bus network of the public transportation system.

Although Montréal is the largest French-speaking city after Paris, it is still unmistakably a big North American city which allows breathing space for the many aspects of cultural development. This can be recognised in the city's art and cultural life. One can experience it while strolling through the streets and above all during walks in the parks.

Montréal / **Sights**

In Le Vieux Montréal, the downtown area of the city, it requires little effort to explore the well-preserved and completely renovated streets and squares of the oldest district of the metropolis. The best starting point is at the route 2 (red) subway station "Champ-de-Mars." To the south lies the *Place-de-Vauquelin* with the statue commemorating the ill-fated French Canadian proponents of 1759/1760. The *Champ-de-Mars* were not only the parade grounds, but also a meeting place and promenade for the people of the past century. Today, this zone has been dedicated to the automobile: Parkareal. Two buildings worth seeing: to the west, the old *Palais de Justice* from 1856 and the *Hôtel de Ville* from 1872 border the square.

On the adjacent *Place Jacques Cartier,* laid out around 1800 and stretching down to the harbour, the Nelson Column commemorates the victory of Trafalgar. Numerous restaurants and sidewalk cafes offer a chance to take a break. All along the way to the harbour, one will come across artists of all kinds. Musicians and jugglers entertain passers-by and a troop of street actors finds its audience. Directly at the beginning of the Place Jacques Cartier, near the Nelson Column on the southwestern corner, is the Tourist Information Centre. Somewhat farther on the same side, number 280 Notre Dame, is the *Château de Ramezay,* the former residence of the Governor, built in 1705. Today, this building houses a museum documenting the historical development of old Montréal.

Farther east along Notre-Dame, one will come upon the *House of George-Etienne Cartier,* 485 Notre-Dame, who was one of the founding fathers of 1867. The complex is comprised of two buildings in the Neoclassic style of the early 19th century. They are open to the public during the summer months.

The Saint-Paul Street then leads back into the old district. The street was named in honour of one of the founding fathers, who was the leader and founder of the "Ville-Marie" religious community. This street is supposed to have been the first trail in the country blazed by Europeans.

At the junction with Rue Bonsecours is the massive chapel *Notre-Dame-de-Bonsecours* which was built from 1657 to 1659. Like other older buildings, It also required extensive renovations after the fire of 1745. It was given the nickname "Sailor's Chapel" because the first seafarers adopted the custom of attending a service here after surviving the sea passage. From the tower rondelle, there is a good view of the old city and the harbour. The small museum, named after the chapel's constructor, Marguerite Bourgeoys, documents the eventful history of the building. Across the way, on the Rue Bonsecours, one will see a row of historical patrician houses dating back to different eras. The *Bonsecour Market* commissioned by the new city administration after the city referendum of 1831, has a dynamic past. It served as a city hall from 1852 and when Montréal became the capital of the united Canada, the parliament was in session here. After Québec became the seat of the Federal Parliament, this served as a market-hall.

The street running parallel, *Sainte-Amable* was the "Fleet Street" of Canada in the past century. No less than six newspaper publishers worked here alongside one another. Lawyers, journalists and authors called this street home. After one has once again crossed the Place-Jacques-Cartier, one will come to the *Centre d'histoire de Montréal* at Place d'Youville number 335, housed in the former fire department. The historical development of the city, which

At home in Canada — the elk with its respect-inspiring antlers

began directly adjacent on Pointe-à-Challières as Ville-Marie, is presented in an easily understood manner. The first log cabins stood here, the riverbank served as the first harbour.

Back on the Rue Saint-Sulpice, which commemorates the first church congregation that once owned the old city district as a result of a royal donation, one will once again come to the *Cours le Royer,* an old warehouse dating back to 1862, built on the ruins of the first hospital. Then one will pass a historical area along the Rue Saint-Sulpice heading north. The patrician houses on the right and left witnessed the city's evolution into a cosmopolitan metropolis. The impressive *Basilica Notre-Dame,* built from 1824-1829, dominates the *Place d'Armes* in the old district. The cathedral in Montréal is an representation of great architecture and artistic design. In the summer, tour guides wait at the entrance and explain various aspects of the cathedral to visitors. Among these are the *Sacré-Coeur Chapel* and the small *church museum*. The western annex is the *St. Sulpice Seminary* dating back to 1685, the oldest remaining stone

Built for the Olympic games in 1976 — the Olympic Stadium in Montréal

building. It is still home to the order; only the wooden clock (approximately 1700) from the bell tower has since been placed in the museum.

To the north, the secular buildings begin. This is Montréal's *Golden Mile,* once the bank district of Canada.

The *Prévoyance Building* from 1929/1930, with its terraced facade and ornate Art Deco lobby, is the first building one will come upon. The next, on the corner of Saint-Jacques Street, is the *New York Life Building,* a red sandstone construction from the year 1888 and Montréal's first "skyscraper." The most impressive is the *Bank of Montréal.* Built in the "pantheon" style, this is the oldest and most significant bank in Canada today. The lobby resembles a Romanic basilica and is renowned for its decor. Those who choose to visit it can view Canada's best coin collection. Admission is free of charge; the collection can only be viewed during banking hours.

The contrast is all the more striking to the *Palais des Congrés,* a futuristic glass palace, which is built on cement columns above the Ville-Marie Expressway. The building is the centre for Canada's most modern data and telematic products.

On Boulevard Saint-Laurent and in the side-streets is the picturesque district of the old *Chinatown.* As is the case with all Canadian cities, during the construction of the railway at the end of the 1860's, Chinese workers were imported, exploited and given meagre wages. Today the renovated district is especially attractive for a stroll by the quaint shops, accompanied by exotic aromas. In the bordering areas, any connection with the past ends abruptly. Rue de Ste. Catherine is *the* shopping street in Montréal. On the new *Place Ville-Marie,* one finds oneself in the centre of the city and its skyscrapers. The Place des Arts, across from the Desjardins Complexes is the centre for art and cultural life in Montréal. Three large modern buildings with the *opera,* the *Grand Ballet Canadien* and the *symphony orchestra* are the working and performing facilities for international artists. At the end of a walk through old Montréal, one will reach the "Place-des-Arts" subway station, route 7 (green). Using the subway one can then set off to explore the *Catacombs of Montréal.* The city built an underground shopping centre in connection with the subway construction. It got such rave reviews from the residents that, today, a completely underground existence is possible, using the subway and travelling in a rectangle: "Place-des-Arts," "Palais des Congrés," "Windsor Station" and "Les Cours Mont Royal."

Even the main VIA Rail train station is included in the underground network. Above ground, there is only a sign, which can easily be overlooked, indicating the entrance on Place Ville-Marie and the Hotel "La Reine Elisabeth," number 900 on Boulevard René-Lévesque Ouest. An approximately 13 kilometre long pedestrian zone runs underground, with more than 1000 stores, 130 restaurants, 25 bank branches and 25 cinemas and theatres. The Métro halls are also examples of modern architecture: each station was designed by a different architect, many decorated with murals or other types of visual arts. The city underground is visited daily by 200,000 people who take advantage of the shopping when using the subway or take advantage of the subway to do their shopping.

Le Mont or — depending on the preferred language — *The Mountain* is a park overlooking the city. From here, one will have a wonderful panorama of the valley and river and a view similar to that which inspired Jacques Cartier to spontaneously call it royal — Mount Royal — 450 years ago. From the observation platform below the large cross, one can see more of the 51 kilometre long island than was possible at Jacques Cartier's time. The rather charming skyscrapers extend all the way to the foot of what remains of a volcano. An impressive view can be experienced at dusk when the city lights twinkle on and the silhouette of the city can still be seen. To the rear, the park stretches along Lake Castor. Bordering on the park is the seemingly endless cemetery of the big city, which, since a long time, has no longer been able to accommodate all of the departed citizens of Montréal. On Ste. Hélène, a remnant of the Expo, *Terre-des-Hommes* is very much worth seeing. Located on the other side of the PQ Route 116 highway is *La Ronde,* an expansive amusement park, reminiscent of Disneyland. Both can be reached by taking Métro route 4 (yellow) to the "La Ronde" station. The abundant night life along the strip happens above ground along the stately Ste. Catherine street. The "nighthawks" meet here in bars, discotheques, pubs and varietés all through the night and into the early morning hours.

The Ile Perrot or *Terrebonne* can be reached via PQ Route 20. The island lies in Lac St. Louis and the medieval lifestyle is presented in a mill in the *Parc de la Pointe-du-Moullin;* a second mill is located to the north on PQ Route 25 on Ile-des Moulins.

Montréal / **Practical Information**

Accommodation

Bed & Breakfast: ''B & B Chez Antonio,'' 101, avenue Northview, Montréal, H4X
1C9, Tel: (514) 486-6910; singles Can$ 28-35, doubles Can$ 35-48.

''Chambre et Petit Déjeuner Bienvenue,'' 3950, avenue Laval, Montréal, H2W
2J2, Tel: (514) 844-5897; singles, Can$ 40, doubles Can$ 50.

''Maison touristique Marbel,'' 3507, boulevard Décarie, Montréal, H4A 3J4, Tel:
(514) 486-0232.

Campsites: Montérégie (Rive Sud et sud-ouest de Montréal): ''Camping Camp
Alouette,'' 3441, de l'Industrie, Beloeil, Tel: (514) 464-1661; 140 places, Can$
17. ''Camping Pointe-des-Cascades,'' 2, chemin du Canal, Point-des-Cascades,
Tel: (514) 455-2501; 54 places, Can$ 15.

Basses-Laurentides: ''Camping Paul Sauvé,'' Route 344, Oka, Tel: (514)
479-8337; 298 places, Can$ 16.25. ''Camping Parc Mont Laval,'' 675, boulevard
St-Martin Ouest, Sainte-Dorothée, Tel: (514) 689-1150; 160 places, Can$ 20.

Hotels: Central: ''Château de L'Argoat,'' 819, rue Sherbrooke Est, H2L 1K1, Tel:
(514) 842-2046; 29 rooms, singles Can$ 45-80, doubles Can$ 50-90, good standards.

''Hôtel Saint-Denis,'' 1254, rue Saint-Denis, H2X 3J6, Tel: (514) 849-4526; 60
rooms, singles and doubles Can$ 40-75, average standards.

''Manoir des Alpes,'' 1245, rue Saint-André, H2L 3T1, Tel: (514) 845-9803; 30
rooms, singles Can$ 45-70, doubles Can$ 50-70, average standards.

''Hôtel le Bristol,'' 1099, rue Saint-Denis, H2X 3J3, Tel: (514) 843-3096; 23 rooms,
singles Can$ 30-120, doubles Can$ 35-125, simple.

''Hôtel Idéal le Sherbrooke,'' 1255, rue Sherbrooke Est, H1B 1C8; 71 rooms,
singles and doubles Can$ 100-125, new hotel.

A number of additional hotels and motels are located to the east and west
of the Ile de Montréal as well as near the Aéroport international de Montréal.
Information and lists are available through the Tourist Information Office.

Youth Hostels/Dormitories

''Auberge Internationale de Montréal,'' 3541, rue Aylmer, Montréal, PQ H2X
2B9, Tel: (514) 843-3317, Can$ 9.50. Non-members Can$ 12.50. The hostel is
located quite a distance north of the older part of the city near the McGill University and the Molson Stadium and can, therefore, only be reached by regional

buses. The nearest subway station is "McGill" on the number 7 subway (green), but is almost one kilometre away.

"Montréal YWCA," 1355, boulevard Dorchester Ouest, Montréal, PQ H3G 1T3, Tel: (514) 866-9941, only for female guests. The building is only two blocks from the VIA Rail train station and the subway station "Place Bonaventure."

"YMCA de Montréal," 1450, rue Stanley, Montréal, PQ H3A 2W6, Tel: (514) 849-8393. Located only one block west of the subway station "Peel," subway number 7 (green), and accepts both male and female guests.

Airports: The Montréal International Airport Mirabel (airport for all international flights) is located quite far outside the city on the mainland in the town of Mirabel. It is connected with the city of Montréal by the 50 kilometre long highway per PQ-Route 15. One cannot reach the airport using public transportation; shuttle service from the bus terminal, Can$ 9 for cross-country buses.

Bus Terminal: The bus terminal for cross-country buses is also located in the city: Voyageur Terminus, 505, boulevard de Maisonneuve Est, Montréal,

The basilica Notre Dame in Montréal impresses visitors with its awe-inspiring architecture

PQ H3A 3E5, Tel: (514) 842-2281. There is a subway station directly in the bus terminal.

Car Rentals: Avis, 1225, rue Metcalfe, Tel: (514) 866-7906. Budget, Main Train Station, 895, rue de la Gauchetière Ouest, Montréal, PQ H3B 2N1, Tel: (514) 866-7675. Hertz, 1475, rue Aylmer, Tel: (514) 842-8537.

Currency Exchange: Banque d'Amérique du Canada, 1230, rue Peel. Compagnie de Fiducie Guardian, 618, rue Saint-Jacques. National Commercial — Devises étrangères, 1250, rue Peel.

Information: Office des Congrès et du Tourisme du Grand Montréal, 1555, rue Peel, bureau 600, Montréal, Québec H3A 1X6, Tel: 1-800-363-7777 (daily from 9 am to 5 pm).

Infotouriste, 1001, rue du Square-Dorchester. Branches: Vieux-Montréal, Place Jacques-Cartier, 174, rue Notre-Dame Est; Aéroport International de Montréal.

Post Office: Station A (general delivery letters/poste restante): 1025, rue Saint-Jacques; Station B: 1250, rue University; Station C: 1250, rue Sainte-Catherine Est.

Restaurants: in Montréal, there is a wide selection of culinary treats (over 3,500 restaurants), the French cuisine is especially well represented. An appropriate selection is listed in the guide ''Le Shopping, les Restaurants, la Nuit,'' which is available through the Office des Congrès et du Tourisme du Grand Montréal (→Information).

Shopping: The main shopping streets in Montréal are the Rue Sainte-Catherine and its neighbouring streets Sherbrooke and Crescent. Boutiques for all tastes (exclusive!) can be found in the above mentioned underground Ville souterraine. Crafts (→Québec, Inuit, Indians) can be found in the Guilde Canadienne des Métiers d'Art Québec, 2025, rue Peel, Tel: (514) 849-6091. To the east, on the Boulevard Saint-Laurent one will come to the centre of the Quartier Latin on Rue Saint-Denis. Here, as is the case on Rue Laurier to the north, there are a number of boutiques which sell mainly unusual and exclusive clothing. Most of the larger stores are open from 10 am to 6 pm; many of the boutiques, however, open at 9:30 am; Thursdays and Fridays, the stores are open until 9 pm and Saturdays they close at 5 pm.

Marché Atwater (built in 1933), 138, avenue Atwater; fruit and vegetable market, shops selling cheese, fish, meat etc. Especially popular on holidays and Saturdays. Open: Monday to Wednesday from 7 am to 6 pm, Thursday and Friday from 7 am to 9 pm, Saturday and Sunday from 7 am to 5 pm.

Marché Jean-Talon, 7075, avenue Casgrain; 120 vegetable merchants, multi-cultural atmosphere. Surrounded by butcher shops, cheese and fish shops etc. Open: see Marché Atwater.

Marché Maisonneuve (built in 1914; only in summer), 4375, rue Ontario Est; historical building, fruit and vegetables from Québec, lovely fountain from 1915 which depicts a market woman with her three children. Open (May to October): see Marché Atwater.

Marché Saint-Jacques (built in 1931, May to October: vegetables, October to April only plants), corner of rue Amherst/rue Ontario; fruit and vegetable market (summer), flowers and plants. Open: see Marché Atwater.

Sports: It would exceed the framework of this guide to list all that Montréal has to offer in the way of sports and recreation. Montréal's attractions range from an amusement park, zoo, wildlife park to swimming, golf, fishing and even winter sports. More detailed information is available through: Le service des sports et loisirs de la ville de Montréal, Tel: (514) 872-6211; Regroupement des organismes de Loisirs du Québec, Tel: (514) 252-3000.

Train Station: VIA Rail Station, 895, rue de la Gauchetière Ouest, Montréal, PQ H3B 2N1, Tel: (514) 871-1331. The train station is located in the centre of the city, Place Bonaventure, and also has a connection to the subway system. One feature of this station: the United States Amtrak trains travel to and depart from here.

Mosquitoes

From mid June up until the first frost around the beginning of August, the mosquitoes in Canada's wilderness can become quite a plague.

One consolation is that they are the basis for the diversity of wildlife. Also one can be certain that one will not notice the mosquitoes much in the towns. There are a number of rules of thumb that will help in overcoming this problem.

Mosquitoes are only obtrusive in humid and wet regions where there is little wind. At windy elevations, on lakes and where the ground is dry, one has little to fear from the mosquitoes.

The proper clothing is a determining factor for ones well being on nights when the mosquitoes are about. Those who depart on an outing in tight jeans deserve what they will get. The mosquitoes can bite through any tight fitting clothing with their sufficiently long and stable proboscis. Therefore, when taking an outing into the wilderness, one should wear loose-fitting clothing, but this should fit tightly around the neck, wrists and ankles. Women are advised to wear loose-fitting trousers rather than skirts or shorts. The trouser legs must fit into the boots or fit closely around the shoe.

Those who would like to enjoy a pleasant evening of fishing should wear plastic gloves and a hat with mosquito netting. One should be able to tighten the netting around the collar. It is not necessary to bring mosquito spray or the like to Canada from home. The repellents available everywhere in the stores, like Muskol, are highly effective. However, because of varying skin sensitivity, caution in the use of repellents is advised. It is good to have along, though, should it become necessary.

Motorway Tolls →*Transportation in Eastern Canada*

Municipal Street Systems

The towns and cities in Canada all have a common street system. Visitors should note the following rules of thumb, then most will have no problems with orientation no matter where one might be.

First Rule of Thumb: All of the avenues run parallel to each other; all streets intersect the avenues perpendicularly. The result is a typical grid system. It does not matter in which direction the grid is laid out, avenues will always run parallel to avenues.

Second Rule of Thumb: The numbering of the avenues and streets begins at the city limits with 1st Avenue or 1st Street. They are then numbered consecutively to the opposite city limit. Sometimes the numbering begins with 101 instead of 1. The first hundred are simply ignored.

Occasionally, a Street will have a proper name. In these cases, the appropriate number of the street is skipped over. In large cities, the main central street is employed to further help in orientation, dividing the city into east and west. The most widely known example of this is probably ''Fifth Avenue'' in New York. The addresses then read ''W. 1st Street'' and ''E. 1st Street.''

Third Rule of Thumb: House numbers follow the street grid; they begin new at each block — but with the street number preceding it. This is yet another aid in orientation, making it possible to know where to look for a house merely from the address. This could cause some problems for visitors from Europe, though. The house number 4101 is not found way out on the outskirts of the city as the four-thousand and first house on a street, but as the first house in the block after 41st Street. Keeping with the example of New York, the address would be: 4101-5th Avenue.

New Brunswick

The province of New Brunswick (NB) is the northernmost of the former New England colonies along the Atlantic coast. Living within its 73,437 square kilometres are 715,000 people; the capital is Fredericton with a population of 44,800. This Canadian province has remained geographically and historically inseparable from the neighbouring state of Maine in the US. The Appalachian mountain range leads through the United States continuing north and far into the eastern region of New Brunswick and falling off to the plateau around the Gulf of St. Lawrence. In the north, the artificial border between the US and Canada cuts through New Brunswick's Notre Dame Mountains. The Appalachian range in Gaspésie are in the province of Québec.

Earlier the fishery on the red sandstone island of Madeleine ensured the livelihood for its residents; today it is tourism

Although the highest summit in the Appalachians is only 820 metres above sea level, meaning this is a sub-alpine mountain range, it is not easily passable. From the US, there are only two roadways worth mentioning leading to New Brunswick and not more than a dozen border crossing points between the US and its Canadian neighbour.

The geographical profile of the province is comprised of three regions. First, the southern Uplands and the Bay of Fundy with the largest city in the province, Saint John. Second, in the north, the adjacent Central Uplands, transversed by the mighty Saint John River and beyond its valley, an almost completely unsettled area of mountains, forest and wilderness with almost no road network. Finally, in the southeast, the fertile Lowlands boarding Nova Scotia, which is the agricultural region of New Brunswick. 85% of the province's land are pristine mountain forests supporting a large amount of wildlife; only 7% are used in agriculture.

New Brunswick / **History**

The cultural development of the province began, of course, with the immigration of the Indians here as well. This is also an aspect that New Brunswick has in common with the other Maritimes because when the Europeans landed, the found what was later to become New Brunswick settled by the Micmac from the Algonkin linguistic family.

The French were the first to arrive. Jacques Cartier had discovered the coast in 1534. With Champlain's first journey in 1604, the French settlement began. He promptly explored the Bay of Fundy and named the rivers and bays. Among these was also the Saint John River, the name taken from the Catholic calendar from the appropriate saint's day, as was a common practice at that time. During the following years, a number of French settlement sprang up all along the coast and even in the regions which belong to Maine today. They were all under the rule of central government of Acadia in Port Royal, today Nova Scotia.

In 1627, the king of France delegated the land at the mouth of the Saint John River to Sieur Charles de la Tour, who established a trading post there. What at first was a neighbourly relationship with the English colony in Boston did not last long. Resulting from the hundred years of armed conflict with England, France was defeated and was forced to give up the entire Acadian region to

England in 1763 in accordance with the Treaty of Paris. The Acadians attempted to flee the ensuing persecution by in the country's interior. With this, the development of the extensive Saint John River valley began, which was only possible due to their traditionally good relations with the Micmac. The English settlement of the region did not happen at first. This changed with the prosecution of the Loyalists resulting from the US's aspired independence. The British troops were able to hold the wooded mountain areas. The present-day border between Maine and New Brunswick resulted from this and thousands of the persecuted Loyalists found refuge in this region. In 1784, the British crown had already made the present-day region of New Brunswick into an autonomous colony, separate from Acadia. It was named after the royal house which ruled England at that time, the Brunswicks (German: Braunschweiger). Around 1840, a potato famine lasting several years broke out in Ireland due to a number of bad harvests. New Brunswick became a favoured destination for those fleeing the famine. Over 150,000 Irish immigrated to the province in the space of a few years. Today, New Brunswick, one of the four founding provinces of Canada in 1867, is the only truly bilingual province. Everything is written in English and French — only historical terms are left untranslated. Thus the correct name of the province is: New/Nouveau Brunswick. All of the civil servants must have a command of both languages because every citizen has the right to be assisted in his or her native language.

New Brunswick / **Economy**

As 85% of the land is forest and mountain wilderness which is not suited for agriculture, the economic emphasis is quite naturally placed on the timber trade and the processing of wood. The second most important economic factor is tourism. In addition to these, fishing also plays an important role because the coastline is far longer than New Brunswick's other border.

Agriculture does play an important role in the Saint John River valley, which is often compared to the Rhine valley in Germany. Its headwaters are found in the border region between the neighbouring state of Maine and the province of Québec. It flows through the entire province from north to south before emptying into the Bay of Fundy.

The lowlands make up an extensive region used for cattle-breeding around Sussex between Saint John and Moncton.

The dispersion of the population is also in accordance with the natural geographical conditions: the river valley, the Lowlands and the coastal regions are the main population centres; hardly anyone lives in the wilderness of New Brunswick's interior.

New Brunswick / **Travelling There**

New Brunswick can be reached from all directions either on the highways or by ferry connections with the other Maritime provinces.

The Greyhound cross-country bus route goes from New York through Boston and along the coastline to Saint John. From Central Canada, New Brunswick can be reached via Montréal — Québec — Edmundston — Fredericton and from the Gaspésie via Campbellton — Fredericton — Saint John, or Moncton — Saint John. One will also travel via Moncton when coming to New Brunswick from Nova Scotia. Moncton is the province's railroad junction. Express passenger trains only serve the route from Nova Scotia via Moncton to Saint John. To continue on to central Canada, the route first leads through Maine, reentering Canada at Sherbrooke/Québec. This is the Trans-Canadian route which ends on the Pacific in Vancouver.

VIA Rail serves the province with two additional passenger routes beginning in Moncton: first, to Edmundston and another via Campbellton and Matapédia to Montréal.

The central airport is located in Saint John, but is only significant in regard to domestic flights.

New Brunswick / **Useful Addresses**

Tourism New Brunswick, P.O. Box 12345, Fredericton, NB E3B 5C3, Tel: (506) 453-2377. The *general informational brochures* for this province are available from this office free of charge.

Department of Natural Resources and Energy, 498 York Street, Fredericton, NB E3B 3P7, Tel: (506) 453-2440. *Hunting and Fishing Information* is available from this office as well as the necessary licences.

Lower Saint John River Promotion Association, P.O. Box 105, Gagetown, NB E0G 1V0, provides informational materials and maps for independently organised *bicycle tours* through the country.

Eastwind Cycle Tours, P.O. Box 1958, Sussex, NB E0E 1P0, Tel: (506) 433-4663, offers the appropriate equipment for independently organised bicycle trips and arranges tours stopping at Bed and Breakfasts along the way.

Lands Branch, Department of Natural Resources, P.O. Box 6000, Fredericton, NB E3B 5H1, will send information on *canoeing* on the rivers in the province free of charge.

The topographical *maps* of the province can be purchased locally at the Department of Natural Resources, Room 575 in the Centennial Building, Fredericton.

Newfoundland

Canada's easternmost province of Newfoundland is comprised of the island bearing the same name and the mainland portion of Labrador. Of the total area of 405,700 square kilometres, 234,330 are in Labrador. Newfoundland has a total population of 580,000 with 40,000 living in Labrador. The capital is St. John's with a population of 85,000.

An idyllic yet rugged beach near Shediac, New Brunswick

The island rises out of the sea like a huge boulder in the Atlantic — the last of the foothills belonging to the Canadian Shield — forming the last boundary of the Gulf of St. Lawrence. The rocky island is distinctly subdivided by its mountain ranges, rocky coasts and countless fjords having a pronounced similarity to the Norwegian coastal landscape. The populations centres are concentrated along the coast, while the interior of the island is for the most part an unpopulated region of mountain wilderness, with forests reaching all the way to the regions near the summits. Only at these altitudes does the tundra begin. The streets, if there are any at all, parallel the coastline; only one transverses the island: the Trans Canada Highway, which finally reaches its terminus at the capital of St. John's. The towns in the southern part of the island and a large number of other towns have no connecting roadways at all and are dependent on ferry connections and transportation by ship. The dependence on ferries is far greater here than in Canada's other Maritime provinces. On the island of Newfoundland, ships are much more important for travellers than automobiles and streets.

Newfoundland / **History**

Based on the sporadic historical finds, it is estimated that Newfoundland was not inhabited 9,000 years ago. Then the first Indians arrived on Newfoundland on their eastward journey; they were most probably the ancestors of the Beothuk, a tribe that has long since died out.

A good deal later, the Micmac Indians followed, having travelled through the Maritimes and populating the southern portion of the island up to the present. The Inuit settled in Labrador's northern coastal region, while the Naskapi inhabited the high tundra of Labrador. Around the year 1000 A.D., the first white races appeared in the waters surrounding Newfoundland. A small Viking settlement was excavated at L'Anse aux Meadows on the northernmost tip of the island. Other archaeological finds support the theory that Vikings from Greenland visited the island regularly. They brought back wood which was lacking in their "Vinland" on Greenland and probably fished and hunted as well. The smooth waters surrounding the island, known as the Newfoundland banks, were doubtlessly the most plentiful fishing areas in the world. It is postulated that fishermen from Europe followed the Vikings' example and that sea passages between Europe and Newfoundland were frequent long before

Columbus. When John Cabot then officially ''discovered'' Newfoundland, having been commissioned by the English crown in 1497, it had already been a destination for European fishing fleets for 500 years. From this time on, England emphasised the ''discovery'' and supported the island, although no colonisation took place at first. The English immigrants preferred to settle further south in what was later to become the United States.

Instead, French fishermen came, who were inevitably drawn into the armed conflict between the two world powers regarding political dominance in the North American continent. The conflict was carried out with gunpowder and lead until Newfoundland was given to England in accordance with a treaty in 1713. Despite this, the actual French settlement of the island began soon after. As a result of the battles in the south, many Acadians from Nova Scotia and New Brunswick fled to the north. Even today, extensive coastal regions are populated by Franco-Canadians. With the conclusive defeat of the French, the English conquest of St. John's in 1762 and the consequent peace treaty of 1763, these regions came under English colonial rule as well.

At the beginning of the 18th century, British (predominantly Irish) immigrants flooded into the country. The English crown established a colony with, in part, independent colonial administration, which was later placed under the sovereignty of the island's parliament in 1855. Then, when the federal state of Canada was founded in 1867, Newfoundland's parliament declined membership in the union. This decision was repeated a number of times until a referendum in 1949 resulted in its incorporation into the Canadian union.

The part of the Labrador peninsula which belongs to Newfoundland, became part of the province more as a result of its geography than political intent. Since the coastal regions of Labrador were inaccessible by any other route but by sea from the Colony of Newfoundland, England transferred control of these mainland regions to Newfoundland in 1809. As Québec evolved, the province gradually expanded all the way to Labrador, while Newfoundland remained an independent English colony until 1949. Considering these historical developments, it is then not surprising that Labrador has ultimately become the object of dispute, which continues even today. The setting of Labrador's borders was the result of a court ruling in the year 1927 — the border runs along the water-shed divide separating the rivers which flow into the Hudson Bay and those which flow into the Atlantic. Québec refuses to recognise this border. Even when Newfoundland joined the union, it did not change this situation. The situation has become so heated, that only in Newfoundland does one speak of Labrador; in Québec it is referred to as Nouveau Québec. In Québec, the tourist must expect that any inquiries Québec regarding "Labrador" will be referred to Newfoundland whether or not the region in question belongs to Québec or not!

Newfoundland / **Economy**

Subsistence and income can be accredited to the seemingly inexhaustible abundance of fish in the Newfoundland banks. Fishing and fish processing was a basis which was presumed to ensure the economy of Newfoundland perpetually. For this reason, the "Newfies'" astonishment was all the more pronounced when one fish processing factory after the other suddenly closed its doors permanently in the late 1980's. There were no more fish in the Grand Banks! This seemed so unbelievable that the workers in the fish industry went on strike because of the lack of fish!

The cause of this was the unchecked pillaging of a number of other countries with modern ships able to virtually vacuum up entire schools of fish with their technically perfect net systems. Environmental pollution also played a role: the contaminated waters of the St. Lawrence River spread around the island, making the island no longer able to support itself from the fishing industry. The time couldn't have been more opportune for the recent discovery of oil off the coast of Newfoundland. A growing number of job opportunities is developing in the oil refining sector. In addition, lumber processing is an economic base in Newfoundland. The province also has a number of ores and mineral resources, the mining of which had remained undeveloped due to the expense involved.

Newfoundland / **Travelling There**

On the island of Newfoundland, there are two airports which are well integrated into the domestic air travel network in Canada: St. John's Airport and Gander Airport. Both are also destinations of a few trans-Atlantic flights from a handful of European airports like London, for instance.

Those who would like to fly to Labrador can fly to Goose Bay. The services offered at this airport are similar to the two mentioned above. One can reach all of the smaller airports on Newfoundland and Labrador. In addition, every larger town in the province will have its own runway, served by the larger airports at least twice a week.

Ferry Connections

The main sea connection is from North Sidney NS Channel — Port aux Basques NF. The ferry offers passenger and automobile transportation during the entire year. Examples of prices for the 5 to 7-hour trip (depending on the type of vessel) are: adults Can$ 13.25 and an additional Can$ 41 for an automobile. The departure times of the two return trips offered daily are changed several times during the year. One should, therefore, check this locally. This ferry line is part of the Trans Canada Highway, making it possible to travel to Newfoundland by bus: to North Sidney with the Acadian Lines, crossing to Newfoundland by ferry (Terra Transport Lines) and continuing to St. John's. There is a second bus route from St. John's to the other ferry harbour of Argentia. The second ferry connection (combined passenger and automobile transportation) starts in North Sidney NS as well. When taking this ferry route, one

Many towns in Newfoundland are widely scattered and are dependent on the ferry connections

travels directly to the Avalon peninsula — the shortest way to the provincial capital. This route, however, does take longer. The trip lasts 19 hours and costs Can$ 36.25 for adults. The ferry is in operation in the summer from June 13 to September 10, once every other day.

Information: Marine Atlantic, P.O. Box 250, North Sidney NS B2A 3M3, Tel: (709) 794-7203, within Newfoundland toll-free: 1-800-563-7701; all other Maritime provinces: 1-800-565-9470. This company runs both ferry lines.

Travelling to Labrador

One can take the automobile and passenger ferry from Lewisporte, a village 60 km north of Gander which can be reached via the Trans Canada Highway and NF Route 340. This ferry stops only once in Cartwright, Labrador and continues to its final destination, Goose Bay, Labrador. The trip takes 32 hours and costs Can$ 61 for adults and Can$ 88 for an automobile. This ferry route is only in operation in summer, twice a week in each direction.

Information can be obtained from the Marine Atlantic office mentioned above. In both towns in Labrador, one can transfer to the coastal ferries offering service to all of the villages north to Nain. These villages are not linked to the roadway network. These ferries can also be boarded directly at Lewisporte. They originate there, make a stop in St. Anthony in the northern part of Newfoundland and continue to the individual villages along the coast of Labrador up to Nain. The ferry mentioned first is an express route which transports automobiles as well. The second is only for passengers. Information on these ferries is also available through the Marine Atlantic office mentioned above. Only one more ferry connection remains to be mentioned. Operated only in the summer, this route is from Province Québec to St. Barbe. The harbour on the island of Newfoundland is linked to the roadway network; St. Barbe is not (if one disregards the 80 km long road to the neighbouring village of Red Bay). For this reason, the ferry does not transport automobiles. Those who would like to bring along a car despite this can obtain information from Relais Nordic Inc., Blanc Sablon, Dup. Co., PQ G0G 1C0, Tel: (418) 461-2656.

Ferries to Saint Pierre-et-Miquelon

There is a further ferry route from Fortune in southern Newfoundland to the harbour of St. Pierre. St. Pierre island and the neighbouring island of Miquelon are the only remaining portions of Canada which are still a French territory. Today they make up a French Department. The only connection to these islands is the above mentioned ferry. The ferry does not transport automobiles.

Newfoundland / **Useful Addresses**

General information about Newfoundland is available through the Department of Development and Tourism, Tourism Branch, P.O. Box 2016, St. John's, NF A1C 5R8, Tel: (709) 576-2830.

Hunting licences and information are available through the Department of Culture, Recreation and Youth, Wildlife, Division, P.O. Box 4750, Building 810, Pleasantville St. John's, NF A1C 5T7, Tel: (709) 576-2815.

Fishing licences and information are available through the Wildlife Division mentioned above. Information on the two *national parks* is available by contacting the Superintendent Gros Morne National Park, P.O. Box 130, Rocky Harbour, NF A0K 4N0, Tel: (709) 458-2066 or Superintendent Terra Nova National Park, Glovertown, NF A0G 2L0, Tel: (709) 533-2801.

Nova Scotia

Like a huge breakwater, the peninsula of Nova Scotia (55,487 square kilometres) extends 560 kilometres in the Atlantic off of the mainland. It shelters not only the neighbouring province of New Brunswick but Prince Edward Island to the north and the entire Gulf of St. Lawrence as well. The gulf has only two sea entrances: the Cabot Strait between Nova Scotia and Newfoundland and the Strait of Belle Isle between Newfoundland and Labrador. Nova Scotia consists of two distinct geological formations. The main portion takes in a low plateau which is connected to the mainland by the Isthmus of Chignecto. It is only on this isthmus that the foothills exceed an altitude of 300 m above sea level. Densely wooded hills, numerous bays and a pronounced subdivision of the coast with fertile valleys characterise this region.

Cape Breton Island is quite different from the eastern portion of this province. The narrow Strait of Canso separates it from the rest of Nova Scotia — a road over a land bridge connects both portions of the province. The island is a rugged barren mountain landscape with peaks ascending to over 554 m above sea level. The rocky coast with its steep, surf-pounded cliffs and fjords are very similar to the Scottish Highlands and the Hebrides. This is an appropriate comparison, as the experts tell us. Long before the first Scottish immigrants arrived, this rocky island broke off of Scotland and, resulting from the continental drift over millions of years, "drifted" to its present-day location across the Atlantic. Thus the name Nova Scotia (= New Scotland) is appropriate in terms of both history and geology. The long, southern Atlantic coastal regions are made up of grey granite cliffs, a steep coastline and numerous bays and fjords: a landscape not suited to agriculture. In the exact middle on one of the largest natural harbours in the world is the provincial capital of Halifax with a population of 115,000. On the northern coast on the opposite side of the peninsula, located on the sheltered Bay of Fundy, is the agricultural region of Nova Scotia. Here, even grapes ripen in the vineyards of the Annapolis Valley. Beyond the Isthmus of Chignecto, on North Humberland Road is the beach resort area of the north. The calm coastal waters and the broad sand beaches warm up to such a degree in summer that a number of beach resorts have sprung up all along the 200 kilometres of coastline, making this the "Costa del Sol" of the Maritimes.

Nova Scotia / **History**

Long before the arrival of the first white visitors, the Micmac Indians (belonging to the Algonkin linguistic family) settled here. Their descendants still inhabit this region today. The first white race with which the Micmac came into contact were the Vikings. As supported by isolated archaeological finds, this region of North America was a destination for the Viking long boats. They came here to stock up on wood — the most important commodity on the treeless island of Greenland.

John Cabot — actually, this man was an Italian named Giovanni Caboto — could hardly overlook the coast of this province on his journey in 1497. His description was, unfortunately, so inexact that, today, one comes upon towns all over the Maritimes which claiming to be the place where John Cabot landed. The only significance of this landing was that Cabot declared English rule over these regions, bringing the British crown into the perpetual conflict with France. The first settlers here were, in fact, French. They sailed in 1605, lead by Sieur de Mont (who had given Henry of Navarra extensive trade privileges) into the same natural basin where the town of Digby (population 2,600) and its ferry harbour are located today. They sailed eastward into the long Annapolis Basin and into the mouth of the St. Lawrence River. The river is made narrower by a pronounced land formation. Here, the newcomers founded Port Royal, the main town in French Acadia for a long period of time. Today, it is a village of 700 named Annapolis Royal.

Then, the appointed King James I of England enfeoffed no less than 140 of his trusted Scottish devotees, giving them expansive tracts of land in Acadia. Thus, Nova Scotia came upon its present-day name: New Scotland. In the years to follow, the same drama typical all over the North American continent took place here as well: the English-French conflict. During the battles and armed conflicts, the more quickly growing British population prevailed. In 1710, Port Royal fell to England and became capital of the English colony. In the Treaty of Utrecht, France ceded Nova Scotia to England in 1713. Only the island of cape Breton remained under French rule. France began developing the Fortress of Louisbourg there into the most powerful bulwark on the continent. During the prelude to the Seven Years' War in 1755, the brutal persecution of the Acadians in the English colony began. In a wild and unbridled orgy of murder and pillaging, the French descendants — and this was their only ''offense'' — were deprived of their rights, bludgeoned and the survivors were packed onto ships and driven out of Acadia.

In 1763, the Treaty of Paris put an end to the Seven Years' War and England granted the Acadians the right to return. As a result, about 10% of the present population of Nova Scotia are Franco-Canadians.

With the dissociation of the New England colonies from the English homeland, the Americans distinguished themselves with a second wave of persecution of an even larger scale. From 1776, a strong influx of Loyalists — refugees and others driven out of the US — into Nova Scotia as well as other provinces. During the following century, the flow of immigrants, largely Scottish continued until 77% of the population was of British descent. Among these were so many Gaelic-speaking people that, it is said, more people in Nova Scotia speak this language than in Scotland itself.

In 1758, Nova Scotia was the first English colony to be granted self-administration. Since then, it is administrated by a government responsible to the parliament. In 1867, Nova Scotia was one of the four founding provinces which brought the Canadian union into being.

Nova Scotia / **Economy**

Earlier, Nova Scotia was reputed worldwide for its ship-building — but this time has ended. It was the period of the great sailing vessels that made Nova Scotia famous. In Lunenburg — the name points to an originally German settlement — the tradition is still fostered. Veteran sailing vessels in need of repairs are renovated on the wharfs, on which the "Bluenose" (once the worlds fastest sailing vessel) was built.

A variety of small industries is now the economic base of the province, followed closely by the income resulting from the tourist industry. In addition, agriculture and fishing as well as the timber industry still play a role in the economy.

Nova Scotia / **Travelling There**

The international airport in Halifax/Dartmouth *(→Halifax)* offers direct flights to many destinations in the US as well as to the European continent. The only roadway is over the Isthmus of Amherst where one changes from the SMT Line buses to the Nova Scotian "Acadian Lines" when travelling by cross-country bus. One can use this bus line to travel to Halifax, continuing to Yarmouth or from Truro to North Sidney and/or (around the Bras d'Or Lake) to Sidney proper. The other route along the southern coast as well as the Cape Breton Region Island are served by small local buses which do not accept the Greyhound pass.

Ferry connections expedite the trip to Nova Scotia, which otherwise would lead around the entire Bay of Fundy when coming from Boston or New York. In summer, the passenger and automobile ferry operates once daily from Portland, Maine to Yarmouth, NS. Information: Prince of Fundy Cruises, Box 609, Yarmouth NS B5A 4B6, Tel: 1-800-565-7900, toll-free when calling from the Maritimes.

From Bar Harbour in Maine, there is a daily ferry connection (passengers and automobiles) to Yarmouth in summer. An additional ferry route is also in operation in summer twice daily from Saint John NB and Digby NS, also for passengers and automobiles.

Examples of prices for the ferry departing from Saint John: adults Can$ 14.25, automobile Can$ 44.

The two other ferries cost Can$ 25.50 for adults and Can$ 47.25 for a car. Information on the latter two ferry connections is available through: Marine Atlantic, Box 250, North Sidney, NS B2A 3M3, Tel: 1-800-565-9470, toll-free when calling within the Maritimes.

Nova Scotia / **Useful Addresses**

General information is available through Nova Scotia Tourism, P.O. Box 130, Halifax, NS B3J 2M7, Tel: (902) 424-5000. This office will send the requested informational brochures about Nova Scotia free of charge.

Hunting licences and information are available through: Department of Land and Forests, 8th Floor, Founders Square, 1701 Hollis Street, Halifax, NS B3J 3M8, Tel: (902) 424-5935.

The Department of Land and Forests, Box 68, Truro, NS B2N5B8, Tel: (902) 426-5952 will give out *information on fishing as well as licences.*

Canoe Nova Scotia, 5516 Spring Garden Road, Box 3010, South Halifax, NS B3J 3G6, Tel: (902) 425-5450 will send information on *canoe routes* in Nova Scotia.

In the Nova Scotia Government Bookshop, 1700 Granville Street, Halifax, all topographical *maps* are available.

Pharmacies

Headache tablets, cold tablets etc. are available without prescription at the pharmacies. Special medication or medication taken regularly (for chronic conditions, for instance) should as a rule be brought along from home in sufficient quantities because these usually require a prescription in Canada. The pharmacies are often either similar or adjacent to a supermarket and, in almost every case, open seven days a week without closing. This service is offered without having to pay higher prices
→*Medical Care*

Postal Service

In Canada, the state-run postal service is responsible only for letters and parcels. All other services are offered by private, profit-oriented companies, with applicable pricing policies. Air mail letters take approximately seven days to reach the addressee and packages take up to four weeks. General delivery letters are conscientiously held — but only for exactly 15 days, whereupon they are returned to the sender! One can have letters or parcels marked ''hold for 15 days'' sent to any post office.

In Canada, the postal codes always consist of the abbreviation for the province *after* the name of the city or town and the subsequent six-digit code (letter-number-letter/number-letter-number). The first three characters consists of the province reference and the sort code; the second combination contains the code for the appropriate post office and delivery district.

Prince Edward Island

Prince Edward Island (5,650 square kilometres, population 128,000) is Canada's smallest province (approximately 0.1% of Canada's total area) located off the eastern coast. The island is in the Gulf of St. Lawrence, to the leeside of Nova Scotia, shielding Prince Edward Island from the Atlantic.

The island's form is that of a elongated half-moon, with its bay to the north. It is 225 km in length and from 6 to 65 kilometres wide, reaching its highest altitude at 152 m above sea level.

The visitor will immediately note the predominantly reddish-brown colour of the sandstone and the island's sandstone cliffs. Rolling hills are quite common in the islands geographical profile. The forests which were reported by the discoverers have long since been deforested. Only groves remain, used to protect against the wind. The reddish-brown, sandy soil, a result of the eroded sandstone which once protruded from the gulf is ideal for the potato crops farmed on 80% of the island's area. Potatoes from P.E.I. are considered to be top-rate agricultural products. these relatively expensive potatoes can be found in all of the finer supermarkets across the continent, even in and especially in the United States. P.E.I is the trademark, resulting from a love of abbreviations characteristic of the North American continent, which also affected the name of the island itself. It is also abbreviated P.E.I. The term "potato island" is not well liked by the islands residents. They prefer to refer to the island as "The Garden of the Gulf." On every local licence plate in P.E.I., the nick-name "Canada's Garden Province" can be found. The favourable natural and climatic conditions of the island resulted in its being the most densely populated region in Canada. P.E.I was the political "heavyweight" among Canada's founding provinces.

Prince Edward Island / **History**

The island was already heavily populated by the Micmac Indians upon the arrival of the first white immigrants. Today, 4,000 Micmac Indians still live on the island. Like many other regions in Eastern Canada, Jacques Cartier was the first to visit and report about this island in 1534.

Cartier named the island "Ile St. Jean," which clung at first. In 1719, the European settlement of the island began. French immigrants sailed into the bay on which the provincial capital of Charlottetown (population 15,800) is now located. They founded Port La Joye across from Charlottetown, near the entrance to the harbour basin. Today, this is the location of Fort Amherst/Port La Joye National Historic Site. As a part of Acadia, this region was also an object of conflict between the English and French rulers. In 1758, the British military occupied the island conclusively. The Acadians were driven out of Acadia. Some fled to the forests, still in existence at that time and remained on the island. Together with the Acadians, who later returned to the island they formed the basis of the present day Acadian population on the island, amounting to 17% of the total population.

Once the fastest sailing ship in the world — the "Bluenose"

The new rulers gave the island an English name: St. John's Island. More far-reaching, however, was the English reorganisation of the islands districts. The surveyor Samuel Holland measured out the entire area of the island, subdividing it into 67 tracts with linear borders, each quadrant with 20,000 Morgens. These were grouped into three counties: Prince, Queen and King County remaining unchanged up to present.

In England, the crown held a unique type of lottery. Wealthy land owners bought lottery tickets, and the winners were drawn — the prizes were the aforementioned lots. With this, the exploitative system of landlords, already notorious in Ireland had been exported to Prince Edward Island. A conflict lasting over one hundred years began between farmers, serfs brought over from England and the landowners in England who siphoned off the profits. It was only in 1853 with the beginning of the land reform that landowners in Europe were forced to sell their land. This process was completed only in 1873 with the founding of the Canadian union. Before this time, the island was a part of the colony of Nova Scotia, which advanced to the status of an autonomous colony later in 1769. In the following years, immigrants from Scotland and the United States flowed into Canada. Potato farming began in 1771 and in 1773, the colonial administration was controlled by a government responsible to the island's parliament. The now prevalent Protestant population wanted to eliminate the Catholic saints from all of the names; thus, the island was officially renamed Prince Edward Island in 1799 after the English prince.

The impulse leading to the founding of Canada came from the politicians of P.E.I. Upon invitation by the island's parliament, the "Fathers of the Confederation" met at Charlottetown. The 23 founding fathers began their deliberations on September 1, 1864. The Dominion of Canada developed out of this on July 1 1867 with permission of the English crown. However, Prince Edward Island first joined this union in 1873 as seventh member.

Membership in the union, however, did not bring the sought-after contact to the mainland. The federal parliament rejected the proposal to build the railroad tunnel in 1905 and the land bridge for the railway, propagated as a substitute never came into being either.

On the other hand, the island stood out because of a number of scurrilous characteristics. Up to 1918, automobiles were legally forbidden and prohibition had already begun in 1906. The island's parliament sustained the prohibition of alcohol up to 1948. It was then replaced with a law that spirits could only be purchased with official government permission. Today, one can buy alcoholic beverages in 15 government-run stores — however, importing alcohol is still strictly forbidden. The tourist is not liable to prosecution, but if a tourist is caught with a can of beer during the extremely unlikely border controls, it will be mercilessly confiscated.

Prince Edward Island / **Economy**

Around 1870, shipbuilding was still an fundamental economic factor. The island's fleet was comprised of 400 deep-sea ships. Nothing remains of these. Today, only small ships are built and maintained. The island's fleet is comprised only of fishing boats which harvest the bounties of the sea from the shallow banks surrounding the island. Cod and herring, tuna and mackerel, lobster and salmon are all offered on the island freshly caught.

Sports fishermen come from all around the world to North Lake as of 1979, a fishing harbour which produced a world record tuna weighing 680 kilograms. The moderate climate and the endless sand beaches also attract avid water sportsmen and swimmers each year, especially from the US. Many of them sail to the protected coast in their yachts. However, those who love long lonely beaches away from the bustle of the beach resorts will still find extensive, deserted sand beaches on which to build their sand castles.

An important economic base is still agriculture with the farming and export of potatoes; however, horticulture and livestock are notably developed as well.

Prince Edward Island / **Travelling There**

P.E.I can be reached by plane by taking a connecting flight from the international airports in Canada. There is quite a respectable airport near the capital of Charlottetown offering daily flights to the airports in the other Maritime capitals. Charlottetown Airport, Brackley Point Road, Charlottetown P.E.I. C1A 6Y9, Tel: (902) 892-3581 (toll-free within Canada 1-800-565-1800) is located about 8 km north of the city and can only be reached by car or taxi. upon landing in Charlottetown, one can take the airport limousine to the downtown area for Can$ 5.

The second option in travelling to Prince Edward Island is by Automobile ferry. There are two combined automobile and passenger ferries from the mainland to Prince Edward Island. The shorter trip of the two is from Cape Formentine

NS to Borden P.E.I. This is also a section of the Trans Canada Highway; duration of the trip is 45 minutes, adults pay Can$ 2.50 and an additional Can$ 6.60 for an automobile. One can also travel the same stretch by Greyhound bus, from Amherst, for example, with the SMT Line to Charlottetown. Bus passengers do not have to pay a fee for the ferry. The train no longer runs to P.E.I. and VIA Rail has even discontinued bus service in 1990.

Information: Marine Atlantic, P.O. Box 250, North Sidney, NS B2A 3M3, Tel: 1-800-565-9470 (toll-free in NS, NB and P.E.I.), otherwise: (902) 538-2278.

These ferries offer shuttle service to and from the island all year; in the summer, 24 hours a day. The second ferry connections is in the south between Caribou NS and Wood Island P.E.I. Duration of the trip is 75 minutes, adults pay Can$ 3.30 and Can$ 10.60 for an automobile.

Information: Northumberland Ferries Ltd., P.O. Box 634, Charlottetown, P.E.I. C1A 7L3, Tel: 1-800-565-0201 (toll-free in NS, NB and P.E.I.) otherwise: (902) 566-3838. This route is only in operation from May 1 to December 20 between

The white houses of Charlevoix, Québec radiate a friendly atmosphere

6 am and 9 pm. The four ferry harbours mentioned are only small villages with limited or no shopping facilities. There are no restaurants on the ferry harbours, but there are on board the ferries.

Prince Edward Island / **Buses**

The state runs the bus company "Island Transit." The main route is in operation all year between Charlottetown and Tignish in the extreme northwest of the island. In summer, the company adds a second route linking Souri in the northeast to Wood Island in the far southeast. During the season, this gives the traveller the option of taking the bus via ferry to P.E.I. from the Acadian Line bus terminal in New Glasgow NS, continuing across the island to Souri and from there taking the ferry to the Madeleine Islands without having to use an automobile. During the trip, the busses stop in every village and, of course, also in Charlottetown.

Prince Edward Island / **Useful Addresses**

General information about the island is available through P.E.I. Visitor Service, P.O. Box 940, Charlottetown, P.E.I. C1A 7M5, Tel: (902) 368-4444 (toll-free on the island: 1-800-565-7421).

Information about *sport fishing* and *fishing licences* is available by contacting the Fish and Wildlife Division.

P.E.I. National Park, District Superintendent, P.O. Box 487, Charlottetown, P.E.I. C1A 7L1, Tel: (902) 672-2211.

Prince Edward Island / **National Park**

The only national park on the island is unique among the 34 protected areas in Canada. It lies in the northern part of the island in the middle section of the coastal region between the beach resorts on Tracadie Bay to the east and New London Bay to the west. It encompasses a narrow strip of coastline 40 kilometres long.

The park is fully developed, contains roads and four campsites run by the park administration (the office is located in the old farmhouse "Green Gables" in the resort of Cavendish in the western portion of the park). The coastal zone, unique even to Canada, is under protection opening to the broad St. Lawrence Bay to the north. Reddish and yellowish sand dunes tower up to 18 metres.

At other places, steep cliffs of reddish sandstone rise up to 30 metres. A broad wall of dunes off the coast forms a perforated, narrow tongue of land, bordering the islands extensive lagoons. A road extends over two-thirds of this tongue of land. Sand dunes, small forests, marshes, ponds, bays and coastal cliffs make up a coastal landscape full of variety, inhabited by innumerous flocks of various species of birds. In addition to patrolled beaches, there are also quiet sections of beach for those who prefer solitude. Golf courses, tennis courts, canoe and sailboat rentals offer more activities in addition to swimming, scuba diving and fishing.

Purchasing Firearms

In contrast to many assumptions, it is not possible to simply go out and purchase a firearm in Canada. Even hunting weapons can only be purchased if the proper documents are presented — and they are then only sent to the customer's home address!

Those who still wish to by a firearm in Canada must have a certificate of good conduct issued by the police in their home country. With this, one can then apply for the permission card to purchase a hunting rifle, valid for five years.

Québec City

Québec, the capital of the Province of Québec, atop the steep left bank of the St. Lawrence River where the river narrows due to a steep, long cliff. At the foot of this cliff, the Rivière Saint-Charles flows into the St.Lawrence. Further downstream, the St. Lawrence broadens, surrounding the large Ile d'Orléans.

Québec City / **History**

Jacques Cartier gave the cliff above the river the name Cap-aux-Diamants, but Samuel de Champlain was the first to found an early settlement here at the base of the 180 metre cliff in 1608. A basic palisade surrounded the first log cabins on the alluvial land where place Royal is located today. Soon, in addition to the fortress complex, the Batterie Royal was built. Later immigrants settled on the island d'Orléans and at other locations. Near the Place Royal, the stone houses of the wealthy bourgeoisie were built. Only gradually did the city spread out to cover the hills that are now the old district of Québec. With the defeat of France after the Treaty of 1713, the construction of Québec's fortifications began. The walls around the old city were built, bastions erected, and finally, the construction of the large fortress complexes on the mound was begun — the present day Citadelle. When the decision was then on the agenda in 1759, only the beginnings of the fortress complex in the style of Vauban were standing.

After the Treaty of 1763, the English continued construction on the fortress. When the US troops, led by Richard Montgomery and Benedict Arnold, attacked the city, Québec withstood.

The US's second attack on Canada, from 1812 to 1814, shocked the English colony so markedly that the fortress was built up to its present-day state. With its five auxiliary stations, Québec became one of the only fully fortified cities in North America. The fortifications never did prove necessary again, however. Under English rule, the city developed into one of the largest shipbuilding and commercial harbours in the world. It is estimated that in Québec, about 2500 ships were built for the British Empire. Parallel to this, Québec served as the seat of the colonial administration. From 1867, it became the capital of the province of Québec.

Québec City / **Sights**

The oldest districts of the city are close together and can be toured quite easily on foot. They are all located within or near the old city walls. Those who would rather not walk can take a horse carriage from Place de l'Esplanade, near the Tourist Information Office. For Can\$ 40 per hour, one can ride in a cab through old Québec. The old city with its cobblestone streets, the small alleyways and broad squares, the sidewalk cafes and cozy restaurants, the historical buildings and the staircases from the upper to the lower city remind the visitor of the old districts of Paris. Strolling pedestrians populate the streets and squares and the atmosphere of Old France is ubiquitous. This part of the city has be continuously under renovations since 1960. In an unparalleled form in Canada, finances have been invested to preserve the old and oppose decay. The ideal starting point for a tour of this city on foot is the square in front of the trademark of Québec, the *Frontenac Castle.* The hotel, one of the most stylish in Canada, has been standing since 1892 where the Governor's Palace once stood. The massive construction with its numerous turrets can be seen from all directions towering over the rooftops. It was in this famous hotel that

Roosevelt met with Churchill to discuss their collective war strategy. It is true
that the ever-popular hamburger can also be purchased in the self-service
restaurant in the lower level of the hotel, but when inside the hotel in the elegant
dining hall and the old-world lobby, the spirit of the turn of the century is still
palpable.

Outside on the corner toward the river is the memorial honouring Champlain,
the founder of the city. From the adjacent *Terrasse Dufferin* there is a magnificent view of the alleyways of the lower city, the river, the harbour, the Island
d'Orléans and the suburb of Lévis. The stairs lead down into the alleyways
of the old district, but one can also take the cog railway which ends at Maison
Jolliet, from the year 1684.

At *Place Royale* was once Champlain's settlement, consisting of only a
warehouse, a store and two residential houses. All around the marketplace
(which was originally called ''Place du Marché'') the renovated houses convey the impression of the centre of New France at that time. The *Notre-Dames-
des-Victoires* church, built in 1688, dominates the one side of the square. It
was damaged twice and then rebuilt in its rather plain architecture.

The alter is in the form of an old fortress with turrets and towers. hanging from
the ceiling is a model of the ship ''Le Brezé,'' which was brought over by the
Marquis de Tracy and the French Regiment Carignan in 1664. The Patrician
houses surrounding the square are an uninterrupted piece of the Middle Ages.
Among these, the *Maison Fornel,* built in 1656, in which the Tourist Information Office is housed today. In the narrow alleyways nearby are numerous old
buildings. Among them is the *Maison Chevalier.* One of its wings, *Frerot,* dates
back to the year 1675. On the whole, the lower city is a rare depiction of a
historical era.

The star-shaped *fortress* on the summit of Cap Diamant resides over the old
city and marks the eastern edge of the city and its fortifications. This is the
garrison of a regiment, the 22nd Royals, but can still be toured daily in groups.
In the former gunpowder storehouse, the *Uniform Museum* is now housed.
Displayed are the military equipment of the 17th century. The military tradition is upheld (to the delight of the visitors) with the ceremonial changing of
the guards, the noontime canons and with the playing of tattoos in the evening. Extending to the southeast of the fortress is the former battle field ''Pleins
d'Abraham,'' on which Generals Wolfe and Montcalm fell and where it was
finally decided in 1759 that Québec would come under English rule. The name

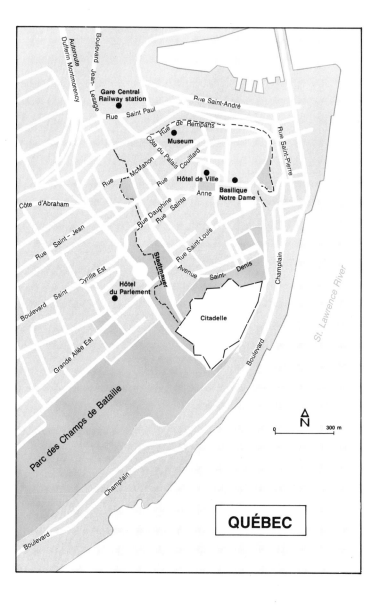

comes from the original owner, Abraham Martin, who acquired the land in 1635. Today, this area is the *Parc des Champs-de-Betaille* and accommodates a number of buildings, for example, the *Musée de Québec,* the *Martello Tower,* a later *fortress,* and the *Wolfe Museum* among others. As the area of this park is very large it is recommended to take a free tour by bus.

If one is now exhausted from the walking, one should retreat to the lower city *Quartier de Petit-Champlain.* Restaurants, small shops, artists and street performers, a lot of colour and a numerous flowers — Petit Champlain is an experience. A small theatre attracts visitors, offering entertainment with a lively programme.

Those who are looking for colourful activity in the upper city will find it on *Place d'Armes,* the former main square and parade grounds in Québec. The sidewalk painters, artists and souvenir merchants clamour in the narrow alleyways around the corner on Rue du Trésor. One can observe everything leisurely from the sidewalk cafes and afterwards, visit the awe-inspiring *Basilica Notre-Dame-de-Québec,* the bishop's cathedral of Québec. The adjacent building, the *Seminaire de Québec,* is the former priest's seminary, which gave rise to the present-day Laval university. This educational centre of Québec is the oldest Catholic institution of higher education on the North American continent. Today, its campus is located in the neighbouring city of Sainte-Foy.

On the opposite side of the Place d'Armes, where an odd looking Gothic fountain has been bubbling since 1816 (it was erected to commemorate the 200th anniversary of the return of the Franciscan monks), is the way to the *Musée de Ursulines.* The former cloister built in 1639 was once the convent of the Ursuline order of nuns. Today it is dedicated to their works. *Old Québec,* within its walls, is almost in every way the ''heart'' of the city. Life pulsates here all year round — even without tourists. In the morning, one meets the residents on the way to the bakery and next door someone else picks up the daily paper. The first guests take a seat in a sidewalk cafe to enjoy their morning coffee, watching the civil servants, late for work, taking leisurely steps toward the governmental institutions. Later, the numerous boutiques, the art galleries and the many small shops and museums open their doors. Then, everything Québec has to offer in terms of lifestyles and other attractions can be experienced in one specific area. Of the many special events during the year, a few are listed here. Two weeks in May are dedicated to an international convention for all types of the performing arts. Street theatre, large stage spectacles and colourful and lively entertainment in the alleyways of the old city attracts the populace into the city, artists, visitors and spectators alike.

In June, modern jazz and blues musicians and fans make a pilgrimage to Québec to applaud the international Avantgarde.

A summer festival for the performing arts brings the people to their feet in July. One of the most significant conventions for performing artists from the French-speaking regions of the world takes place; even the squares in the old city are transformed to stages. ''Expo-Québec'' in late August is then more a trade and export exhibition with a number of shows and other events taking place peripherally.

Quebec City / **Excursions**

By Ferry to Lévis

The trip by ferry from the base of the old city, the Quartier Petit-Champlain, to Lévis is an impressive tour. Lévis also has a number of formidable patrician houses on Rue Guenette, on Avenue Mont-Marie and above all on Rue Wolfe where the ''Centre d'Art de Lévis'' is also located. The small city was named after the duke of Lévis, the French victor in the battle of Sainte-Foy in 1760. If one returns with the ferry which has linked the two cities since 1816, one will have one of the most beautiful views of Vieux-Québec with the dominant facade of the hotel ''Château Frontenac,'' which is even more impressive at dusk when the lights in the hotel and in the lower city are lit.

Parc Cartier-Brébeuf

Another short trip leads through the middle of the metropolis, to 175 Rue de L'Espinay, where the small Parc Cartier-Brébeuf (a national historic park) along the banks of the Rivière Saint Charles awaits the visitors. On the riverbanks is a replica of the ''Grande Hermine,'' the boat with which Cartier sailed to Québec in 1535.

To the Indian Regions

A visit to the first Huron settlement, 1625 rue Notre-Dame in L'Ancienne-Lorette leads through old Québec. In the centre of the small city where the airport of Québec is located today, was once a Seigneurie, that the Jesuits had claimed. When the defeat of the Hurons by the Irokee seemed apparent, the Huron tribes sought refuge within the city walls of their French ally. The Jesuits established a group of the Hurons and built a chapel — or rather, they had the

Indians build one. The name is still used to refer to two suburbs of Québec, it was called "Notre-Dame-de-Loretto, built in 1674. Today, the church "Eglise de L'Ancienne-Lorette" stands in its place, built from 1907 to 1910.

In 1697, the Hurons left the city and from then on settled in Wendake or "Village-des-Hurons," as the reservation is called today. It can be found on Rue Huron No. 25 in Wendake where one can gain an impression of the modern big city Indian. In the heart of this settlement is the new "Notre-Dame-de-Loretto," chapel, now over 250 years old. The reconstructed Indian village is, of course, only an outdoor museum, but one can still form a picture of the original lifestyle.

Ile d'Orléans

Those who have seen enough churches and saints, should gain an impression of the simple country life of the new French-speaking Americans by taking a tour around the Island d'Orléans in the St. Lawrence River. Around 7,000 people live in the tranquil idyll of a garden before the gates of the metropolis. Numerous old buildings call to mind times gone by and in the Moulin Gosselin mill, originating from the year 1635 (number 758 in Saint-Laurent).

Montmorency Falls

Before one rides over the Pont de l'Ile bridge to the island (Cartier called it "Isle de Bacchus") to take advantage of an island tour, one has the chance to experience the marvellous waterfalls of Montmorency only slightly north of the bridge. Some will find these waterfalls more beautiful than the better marketed Niagara Falls, and these are also higher. The water of the Monmorency River plunges 83 metres.

Basilica Sainte Anne de Beaupré

Also only a few kilometres farther north of the Bridge to Ile d'Orléans is the Basilica Sainte-Anne-de-Beaupré, *the* place of pilgrimage in North America since the 17th century. In the fulfillment of an oath, a chapel was built over the river. During its construction, a handicapped worker was healed and the reputation of the building as a place of miracles spread. The chapel was already replaced by a stone church in 1676 and since 1923, massive basilica, built in romanic style, keeps watch from the cliffs over the St. Lawrence River. The impressive modern construction's stained glass windows are especially magnificent, which should definitely be experienced on a sunny morning or afternoon.

In the Château Frontenac, towering majestically over Québec, Roosevelt and Churchill once met to discuss their joint strategy during World War II ▶

The overall picture of the thousands of tourists (over a million annually) who visit the church daily is also colourful. One must consciously overlook the tacky by-products which, seemingly by some law of nature, always accompany such sites of pilgrimage. It is also a spectacle of colour when the Indians meet and mix among the visitors at the beginning of summer or when the gypsy tribes of North America meet here in mid-summer.

In the Rivière Sainte Anne Valley

In summer, the short side-trip into the Rivière Sainte-Anne Valley highly recommended. At the base of the canyon awaits an impressive scene of the rugged backdrop of the cliffs and the frothing current. The falls are 74 metres high in total. Two pedestrian bridges make viewing the falls from a number of perspectives possible. The valley is a five minute drive on Route 138 from Beaupré.

Parc de la Jacques Cartier

Certainly among the tours most worth experiencing in the region around Québec City is a day trip to the nearby Parc de la Jacques Cartier. This is *the* opportunity to gain an impression of the heights of the Laurentide massif (approximately 1000 metres above sea level).

The park is directly outside the gates of the city, only 35 kilometres from the old city. One can reach the park via PQ Route 175, a well paved highway which runs along the border to the park but directly through the surrounding natural reserve (''Réserve Faunique des Laurentides'') into the northern regions of the province of Québec.

Information: Parc de la Jacques Cartier, Bureau d'accueil, C.P. 10 000, Stoneham, PQ G0A 4P0, Tel: (418) 848-3169.

Québec City / **Practical Information**

Accommodation

Campsites: ''Campground Aéroport,'' 2050 route del'Aéroport, Ste-Foy, QC G2E 3L9, 7 kilometres from Québec, 130 places, Can\$ 16 per place and 2 persons, open from the middle of May to the beginning of October.

''Campground Municipal de Beauport,'' 95 rue Sérénité, Beauport, QC G1E 6P4, 6 kilometres from Québec, 130 places, Can\$ 10-15 per place, open from June to September.

''Campground de la Joie Enr.,'' 640 Georges Muir, Charlesbourg, QC G1H 7B1, 8 kilometres from Québec, 105 places, Can$ 12-16 per place, open from the middle of May to the middle of September.

''Campground L'Egaré Enr.,'' 1069 route 138, C.P. 35, Neuville, QC G0A 2R0, 25 kilometres from Québec, 62 places, Can$ 11-15 per place and for three people, open from the middle of May to the middle of September.

''Campground Plage Germain,'' 7001 boulevard Fossambault, Lac-saint-Joseph, QC G0A 3M0, 20 kilometres from Québec, 604 places, Can$ 22 per place, open from May to September.

Hotels/Motels: ''Le Roussillon,'' 339 rue de la Couronne, Québec, PQ G1K 6E6, Tel: (418) 649-1919, 159 rooms, singles and doubles Can$ 75-115, high standards.

''Hôtel Le Gîte,'' 5160 boulevard Wilfried Hamel Est, Québec, PQ G2E 2G8, Tel: (418) 871-8899, singles Can$ 45-90, doubles Can$ 49-100, high standards.

''Hôtel Château Bellevue,'' 16 rue Laporte, Québec, PQ G1R 4M9, Tel: (418) 692-2573, 57 rooms, singles Can$ 54-89, doubles Can$ 59-89, in the off season Can$ 45-65/50 70 respectively, above average standards.

''Motel Royal,'' 1515 boulevard Wilfried Hamel, Québec, PQ G1N 3Y7, Tel: (418) 681-6108, 18 rooms, singles Can$ 61-65, doubles Can$ 70-75, above average standards.

''La Manior Lafayette,'' 665 Grande Alée Est, Québec, PQ G1R 2K4, Tel: (418) 522-2652, 12 rooms, singles Can$ 49-64, doubles Can$ 54-74, in the off-season Can$ 28-43/33-53 respectively, average standards.

Inexpensive Hotels:

''Hôtel Manoir La Salle,'' 18 rue Sainte-Ursule, Québec, PQ G1R 4C9, Tel: (418) 647-9361, 9 rooms from Can$ 23.

''Hôtel La Maison Demers,'' 68 rue Saint-Ursule, Québec, PQ G1R 4E6, Tel: (418) 692-2487, 8 rooms from Can$ 25.

''Hôtel Maison du Général,'' 72 rue Saint-Louis, Québec, PQ G1R 3Z3, Tel: (418) 649-1905, 9 rooms from Can$ 28.

''Hôtel Manoir sur le Cap,'' 9 avenue Sainte-Geneviève, Québec, PQ G1R 4A7, Tel: (418) 694-1987, 14 rooms from Can$ 30.

''Hôtel Manoir de la Terrasse,'' rue Laporte, Québec, PQ G1R 4M9, Tel: (418) 694-1592, 7 rooms from Can$ 34.

''Hôtel Maison Acadienne,'' 43 rue Sainte-Ursule, Québec, PQ G1R 4E2, Tel: (418) 694-0208, 27 rooms from Can$ 34.

"Maison Sainte-Ursule, " 40, rue Sainte-Ursule, Quebec, PQ G1R 4E2, Tel: (418) 694-9794, 15 rooms from Can$ 35.

Youth Hostels/Dormitories: "Auberge de la Paix," 31 rue Couillard, Québec, PQ G1R 3T4, Tel: (418) 694-0735. Located near the city hall in the lower part of the inner city.

"Centre international de séjour de Québec," 19 rue Sainte-Ursule, Québec, PQ G1R 4E1, Tel: (418) 694-0755. Can$ 8 for members, Can$ 9 for non-members. Located in the old city centre midway between the "Voyageur Terminal" and the Citadel, across from the "Québec City Region Tourism Bureau" (see "Information" below).

"Québec YWCA," 855 avenue Holland, Québec, PQ G1S 3J5, Tel: (418) 683-2155.

Airport: Québec City Airport, Route de l'Aéroport, Tel: (418) 692-1031, located 30 kilometres west of the centre of the city in the L'Ancienne-Lorette area. Only domestic connecting flights; it can be reached from the city with bus number 80.

Bus Terminals: The bus terminal for the "Voyageur Lines" cross-country buses, serving the province of Québec in place of the Greyhound Lines, is located directly near the city centre: 255 boulevard Charest Est, Québec, PQ G1K 3G9, Tel: (418) 524-4692. The bus terminal for the city's regional transportation network is around the corner: commission de Transport de la Communauté urbaine de Québec (CTCUQ), Complexe Jacques Cartier, 325 rue du Roi, Québec, PQ G1K 8E9, Tel: (418) 627-2511. It is the most expensive bus service in a Canadian city. The standard price with or without transfers is Can$ 1.25. There are no multiple tickets offered for less. There are no streetcars or subway.

Information: Québec City Region Tourism and Convention Bureau, 60 rue d'Auteuil, Québec, PQ G1R 4C4, Tel: (418) 692-2471.

Train Station: VIA Rail Station, Gare du Palais, 450 rue de la Gare-du-Palais, Québec, PQ G1K 3X2, Tel: (418) 524-6452.

Québec / Province

Canada's oldest Province of Québec encompasses the entire eastern Canadian land mass north of the Ottawa and St. Lawrence rivers. It has an area

As if the clock were turned back — a carriage ride through the Old French alleyways of Québec ▶

of 1,540,689 square kilometres and a population of 6.6 million. South of the St. Lawrence River, the lowlands along the river also belong to the province up to the US border and including the Gaspésie out to the Gulf of St. Lawrence. To the west the 79th line of longitude forms the artificially drawn western border with Ontario. In the east, the portions of Labrador east of the watershed divide belong to the neighbouring province of Labrador; the western portion, to Québec. Physiographically, the province is a part of the Pre-Cambrian Laurentian mountain range as long as these regions lie north of the St. Lawrence River. The mountains have long since been eroded to sub-alpine elevations, ascending quickly from the river valley north to a plateau approximately 1000 metres above sea level and then falling off to the Hudson Bay basin and its southern tip, James Bay.

This region is not suited to agriculture. An endless area of Nordic forests, huge lakes and extensive lake basins characterise this region — a wonderland of pristine, uninhabited landscapes, which has, unfortunately, fallen victim to commercial magnates and politicians. *(→James Bay Project).*

Almost the entire population of the province is concentrated south of this region, in the lowlands of the St. Lawrence River Basin. The settlement of this region began on the fertile soil on both sides of the river. This is the location of the two largest cities Québec and Montréal, which alone account for over 50% of the population of the province.

Québec / **History**

When the first Europeans appeared along the St. Lawrence River, they were received in friendship by the Indians who had long since lived here in large settlements, farming the land. The French settlement was only successful thanks to the help of the natives. This readiness to help demanded reciprocity, and soon France found itself entangled in a cumbersome war with the Irokee, a tribe which enjoyed the support of the English.

Parallel to this, a faithful reproduction of the French homeland gradually grew. Noblemen were given extensive tracts of land, considering it cost nothing. They were, however, forced to import serfs, to draw profits from these tracts. Because of this, only very few Frenchmen came to Canada voluntarily, while in the ''more liberal'' English settlements, the population increased steadily.

Mission work with the aim of converting the Indians was considered a priority from the beginning. Bigotted attitudes were prevalent at the court of Versailles;

thus, ensuring generous financial support for those intent on converting heathens. Two Catholic orders, the Récolets (Franciscans) and the Jesuits quarrelled with abandon over the conversion of the natives and disciplining the immigrants. Extensive privileges and the donation of land made them wealthy in the process. If the power of the Church was great under French rule, then it became even greater when England came into power in 1763.

From this time, the priests had the say in the community, and consequently, a distinctive Franco-Canadian culture developed. In 1774, the British crown granted regional freedom just in time to strengthen the bonds of this population and to immunise them against the revolutionary tendencies in what was later to become the United States.

With the formation of the Canadian state, the former colonial structure of Lower Canada was given its current name. The Franco-Canadian culture could now spread unhindered. Today Québec is the only solely French-speaking province. School French is the official language, but the population speaks a dialect originating from the Middle Ages, which is called "Joual" or "Québecois," quite unintelligible to the European ear. The secession from the Canadian Union, which is repeatedly deliberated publicly, but has never been acted upon, will probably never become a reality. The population has already clearly voted for Canada. Not only the 7,000 Inuit, the 77,000 Indians and Métis, and the 12% Anglo-Canadians in Québec — but also the 83% Franco-Canadians know that they are in good hands in the Canadian Union.

Québec / **Economy**

Of the twelve Provinces of Canada, Québec is the most affluent and economically stable. This is not due to the famous mineral resources and precious metals. These are present in Canada's other regions as well — but no other province is located so favourably in terms of transportation, only a short distance from the world's industrial centres.

The extensive forestry on the Pre-Cambrian shield is a stabile economic factor. No less than 60 gigantic paper mills process over 7 million tons of paper annually, exported worldwide mainly for the production of newspapers. The mining industry makes extensive use of minerals like titanium, quartz, copper, zinc, iron and so on. Even with gold, production is 20% of the Canadian totals and asbestos is 30% of that produced worldwide.

A decisive economic element is the service industry. The harbours of Québec and Montréal, Trois Rivières and Rimouski are forwarding harbours which are leading in the world for container trafficking due to their location on the St. Lawrence River. In the regions surrounding these cities, the service sector has profited from this favourable location on the main traffic artery in Canada. Freight forwarding and distribution for the whole of Canada ensure employment in Canada's metropolises, which evolved here for this very reason.

Québec / **Useful Addresses**

General and supplementary information is available through Tourisme Québec, P.O. Box 20 000, Québec, PQ G1K 7X2, Tel: (418) 873-2015.

Information on *hunting and fishing* as well as the appropriate licences are available through the Ministère du Loisir, de la Chasse et de la Pêche, Direction des Communications, 150 boulevard Saint Cyrille Est, Québec, PQ G1R 4Y3, Tel: (418) 643-3127.

Information on *Parks and Wildlife Reserves* is available through the Ministère du Loisir, de la Chasse et de la Pêche, address: see above.

From the Division des réservations, C.P. 1010, Québec, PQ G1K 8X4, one can obtain information regarding cabin rentals in the parks.

Railway →*Transportation in Eastern Canada*

Radio and Television

Those travelling by car who notice that the car radio has suddenly gone silent, need not think that the radio is defective. They have merely left the radio station's reception area. One will not be able to receive the radio signal until approaching the next town — at least not on an AM/FM radio. In Canada, there are also radio stations which transmit nationwide but only on long and short wave frequencies. Car radios are usually not equipped to receive these. The local transformers in the individual towns are necessary to receive the signal on an AM/FM radio. For this reason, it is not uncommon for the radio to go silent for hundreds of kilometres, even longer in the remote areas of wilderness. In addition to the public radio stations, every town has at least one private station financed through advertising. Therefore, the area of transmission is limited to the town. Conspicuous signs along the roadway furnish information on the frequencies and call letters of the local radio stations. The programmes are interrupted by advertising but also include information of interest to tourists. During the morning hours, classified ads are usually broadcast as a free service of the radio station. The radio is a substitute for the classified advertisement section of the nonexistent newspapers — or it supplements the newspapers in the big cities. Those who wish to sell used merchandise simply call the station. Those wanting to purchase something offered can call the seller. This also works the other way around: tourists who would like to purchase an inexpensive used canoe can call the station to get offers from the radio audience.

Those who would like to be able to receive radio uninterrupted nationwide, must bring along a small short-wave radio. with this one can even receive international stations and stay abreast of the latest events in one's home country. Television is an emphasised form of communication even in the northernmost regions of Canada. In addition to the two national CBC programmes in Canada, there is a number of private local stations. These can not only be received in all of the cities by cable, but also in the most remote Inuit village on the polar sea. The new technologies make satellite reception from the US and Canada possible with a satellite dish.

Restaurants

The simple Canadian restaurants offer inexpensive food. All across Canada, one will find breakfast offered for Can$ 1.99; in the sumptuous restaurant around the corner it can cost Can$ 8. Lunch and dinner can be had everywhere starting at Can$ 5 to Can$ 8, where there is no limit to the prices in the upper categories. One should by all means pay attention to two typical offers: the salad bar, usually well-stocked with a number of other extras like soups, for which one pays a set price and then is free to help oneself to as much as he or she wishes; the lunch specials for a set price: "all you can eat" usually for about Can$ 5. One may then help oneself to as much as he or she wishes from the buffet.

In restaurants, alcoholic beverages are only available if the restaurant displays the sign "full licensed." In the rural regions, these are the only available source for alcoholic beverages. Only in those restaurants displaying the sign "off sales" is one allowed to take alcoholic beverages off the premises — since every possible activity having to do with alcohol must first be licensed in Canada. As the restaurants are only allowed to purchase alcohol from the nearest liquor store (open to the general public) the prices are high. Due to the liquor pricing policies and consumer taxes which vary from Province to Province, the prices quoted here give a general idea: a can of beer will cost about Can$ 3 in the restaurant, about Can$ 1 in the Liquor Store and somewhere between these two prices in an "off-sales" restaurant. A bottle of vodka, the least expensive "strong" in the country, is available from Can$ 20 in the liquor store.

Saint John

Saint John is a significant harbour town and the largest economic centre in the Province of New Brunswick. The "biggest small town in the east" (as the residents quite appropriately call their city) has a population of over 75,000 and is located on the peninsula at the mouth of the Saint John River, which the city surrounds like a lobster claw. The city centre is located to the east on the peninsula between the river and Courtenay Bay.

Saint John / **History**

Although Samuel de Champlain explored this region extensively in 1604, it remained unsettled during the times of Acadia. Some trading posts on the coast were repeatedly pillaged and destroyed by pirates from the New England provinces. Thus, this wonderful natural harbour remained unused for the time being. This first changed when, in the newly established United States, the Loyalists were prosecuted, driven out and their property confiscated.
On May 18, 1783 an entire fleet of fleeing Loyalists, comprised of seven ships in search of a new home, sailed into the mouth of the Saint John River. They founded the present-day city overnight, in the literal sense. 2,000 people are said to have landed here at that time. Thousands would follow in the consequent years. In 1785, Saint John was the first Canadian city to be officially constituted by royal decree. With the arrival of the Loyalists, the turbulent development into a harbour city with shipbuilding, a trading fleet and a remarkable turnover of merchandise began. A short time later, the harbour with its fleet measured according to tonnage was the fifth largest in the world. With the influx of Irish in the period around the middle of the century, the city reached its present size. After this, the growth stagnated and the structures

of the founding period remained, for the most part intact, as long as no fires took place.

Saint John / **Sights**

Four hiking paths which lead through the city, will take visitors to the historical buildings and sites. The oldest residential building is located in the centre of the old district, the *Loyalist House,* kept in the basic Georgian style of 1816. Nearby, adjacent to King Square, is the former *cemetery,* now *city park,* in which the old grave stones still protrude from the grass. The *Prince William Street,* with its old buildings is protected as an architectural monument. The historical *City Market* from 1876 is probably the oldest of its kind on the American continent still used as a marketplace — a forerunner of the contemporary shopping malls. The impressive *Saint John Stone Church* (1825) on a hill overlooking the old city was the first stone building built with ballast stones brought over from England. The modern Market Square on the harbour incorporates the remains of old warehouses, this modern mall combines old with new. Among the numerous shops under this one roof, the *Grannan's Fish House* stands out from the rest. The vaulting of this restaurant's ceilings date back to 1855. In this old restaurant a ''Clam Chowder'' is a special treat.

Fort Howe belongs to the category of very old relics. It is a log cabin from the year 1777, in North Saint John, located on Main Street with a beautiful view of the harbour. Of course, Samuel de Champlain has not been forgotten. A monument has been erected in his honour; his statue looks ponderingly over the city on the corner of Charlotte Street and Queen Square in the southern part of the old city. *The* attraction of Saint John is definitely the *Reversing Falls,* a spectacle of nature which can be credited to the effects of the tides in the Bay of Fundy. During low tide, the water in the Saint John River falls about five metres over the threshold of rocks at the narrow point in the harbour. With high tide, the waterfall is flooded — and the current of the Saint John River is reversed for over an hour — upstream! One can best observe this natural phenomenon from the bridge, on which the NS Route 100 crosses the river. In the Visitor's Bureau (see below) one can obtain the tide schedule so that one can be at the bridge at the correct time of day.

Museums worth seeing are the *Military Museum,* housed in the Carleton Martello Tower, a restored fortification tower (Fundy Drive at Whipple Street,

Tel: (506) 648-4011), and the *New Brunswick Museum.* This is the oldest Museum in Canada and is located somewhat outside the city centre (277 Douglas Avenue).

Saint John / **Practical Information**

Accommodation

Bed & Breakfast: ''Cranberry's B & B,'' 168 King street, Saint John, NB E2L 1H1, open all year, singles Can$ 40 and doubles Can$ 50.

''Dufferin Hall B & B,'' 375 Dufferin Row, Saint John, NB E2M 2J7, open all year, singles/doubles Can$ 50/60, off-season Can$ 32/37.

''Five Chimneys Bed & Breakfast,'' 238 Charlotte Street West, Saint John, NB E2M 1Y3, open all year, singles/doubles Can$ 40/45.

Campsites: ''Rockwood Park,'' Box 7023, Saint John, NB E2L 4S4, Tel: (506) 652-4050, 50 places.

''Seaside Tent and Trailer Park,'' St. Martin's, E0G 2Z0, Tel: (506) 833-4413, located 30 km north of the airport, 75 places.

Hotels/Motels: ''Anchor Light Motel,'' 1989 Manawagonish Road, Saint John, NB E2M 5H6, Tel: (506) 672-9972, 15 rooms, singles/doubles Can$ 29/36, in the off-season Can$ 25/32.

''Colonial Inn,'' 175 city Road, Box 2149, Saint John, NB E2L 3T5, Tel: (506) 652-3000, 96 rooms, singles/doubles Can$ 68/74.

''Hillcrest Motel,'' 1315 Manawagonish Road, Saint John, NB E2M 3X8, Tel: (506) 672-5310, 10 rooms, singles/doubles Can$ 40/46.

''Howard Johnson Hotel,'' 400 Main Street, Chesley Drive, Saint John, NB E2K 4N5, Tel: (506) 642-2622, 100 rooms, singles/doubles Can$ 84/94, in the off-season Can$ 59/69.

''Seacoast Motel, '' 1441 Manawagonish Road, Saint John, NB E2M 3X1, Tel: (506) 672-6442, 13 rooms, singles/doubles Can$ 45/55.

Lodging-house: ''Saint John YWCA/YMCA,'' 19-25 Hazen Avenue, Saint John, NB E2L 3G6, Tel: (506) 652-4720, located on the hill in the old district of the city above the train station. Saint John has no Youth Hostel.

Airport: The Saint John Airport is located at 4180 Loch Lommond Road, Saint John, NB E2N 1L7, about 15 km east of the downtown area and can be reached by bus route 22.

Buses: the SMT terminal for cross-country buses is at 360 Union street, Box 6910 Station A, Saint John, NB E2L 4S3, Tel: (506) 658-6565. It is located in the downtown area.

Saint John Transit connects the suburbs with the downtown area, the buses meet at Kings Square. From Fredericton, the Trans Canada Highway continues along the river, but on the other side of the river in the north.

It then leads over the flatlands by Grand Lake, a large lake with bays and adjacent lakes, continuing east to Moncton and Nova Scotia and, by means of ferry connection, to Prince Edward Island.

Golf: Riverside Country Club, Tel: (506) 847-7545. Rockwood Park Golf Club, Tel: (506) 658-2933. Westfield Golf & Country Club, Tel: (506) 757-2250.

Information: Visitor and Convention Bureau, P.O. Box 1971, Saint John, NB E2L 4L1, Tel: (506) 658-2990. One will find it on the 11th floor of the city hall on King Street near the harbour.

Train Station: The VIA Rail Station is located to the north in the valley directly below NB Route 1; 125 Station Street, Saint John NB E2L 4X4.

The train station cannot be reached using the public bus system, but it is only 500 metres from the bus station and only 200 metres from the YMCA.

Shopping

The larger Canadian cities have numerous shopping malls, some underground, as is the case with Montréal's "Underground City," a 22 kilometre long network with over 1,400 boutiques, 2 department stores, 150 restaurants and 30 cinemas.

Alcoholic Beverages

Alcoholic beverages are expensive in Canada. They can be purchased only in the state-operated liquor stores which are located outside of the cities. One can buy liquor only in the supermarkets in Québec. In restaurants, liquor is available only when the restaurant is identified as "fully licensed;" Liquor can only be removed from the premises if "Off sales" are specified *(→Restaurants)*.

Arts and Crafts

The provinces are known for their excellent craftsmanship in ceramics, weaving, carving, glass blowing and puppet-making among others. Indian and Inuit articles can especially be recommended, however, one must be cautious when purchasing these because many of the articles are mass-produced in Taiwan.

St. John's

St. John's (population: 84,000) is the capital of the province of Newfoundland. The establishment of this city can be credited to the strategical location and the protected harbour basin at the mouth of the Waterford River, which was the haven for the storm-tossed wooden ships sailing in from the Atlantic in the eastern portion of Newfoundland. The basin of St. John's Harbour (also the original name of the city) is similar in shape to a banana. This offered the ships calm waters in which to lay anchor, and the entrance to the harbour ''The Narrows,'' overlooked by the massive ''Signal Hill'' was soon equipped with fortifications and cannons, protecting the harbour from enemies and pirates. Today, the complex is protected as a *Natural Historic Site* and provides a realistic picture of a bygone era. The fortress was the setting of the prolonged conflict between France and England. In 1669, 1705, 1708 and 1762, the fortress was fought over fiercely, finally falling under England's control in a way which was uncannily similar to that of Québec. There, the British General Wolfe took the fort in a surprise attack. Similarly, Colonel Amherst by-passed Signal Hill and the cannons in the defences on Quidi Vidi Lake. He landed his troops on September 13, 1762 north of St. John's in Torbay and had won the battle before it had even begun.

If one disregards the few high-rises on the edge of the harbour in the downtown area, then this, the oldest harbour on the American continent has a more provincial atmosphere. The residential areas are expansive; the houses scattered around the landscape. Towering above their roofs are the two impressive white towers of the Anglican basilica *St. John Baptist.*

In the northern part of the city centre which survived the devastating fire of 1882 unscathed, the *Memorial University of Newfoundland* lies at the foot of the extensive *C.A. Pippy Parks.* The university has been in existence since 1949 and was moved to this campus in 1961. The university shares its campus with the *Arts & Culture Centre,* which was added in 1967. This comprehensive centre houses theatre and concert facilities, museums and art exhibitions. Bordering the university to the east on Prince Philip Drive is the *Confederation Building.* Its doors were opened in 1960, and it is here that the provincial government and administration are housed. Situated on the Kings Bridge Road is the *Commissariat House,* a building from the year 1818, constructed and furnished in the Georgian style of that time. Caretakers in historical costumes lead tours through the building.

The *Colonial Building* on the Military Road was the governmental seat from 1850 to 1960. White sandstone was imported from Cork in Ireland especially for this building, which houses the collection of historical documents and the governmental archives today. Admission is free of charge.

The *Newfoundland Museum* on Duckworth Street preserves the historical artifacts and archaeological finds from the 900 years of historical settlement of Newfoundland. Among these are the relicts already mentioned from the Beothuk culture. Admission is free of charge here too, which is true of all other sites in Québec as well! And for those with a taste for military history: in the Signal Hill National Historic Park, atop a mound between the Atlantic and the harbour is the *Queen's Battery* from 1796. From mid July to the end of August, the ''Signal Hill Tattoo,'' the battle of 1762, is reenacted in historical costumes. In addition, visitors will find old barracks, already converted into a hospital at that time, the place where Marconi sent the first wireless telegram on December 12, 1901, proving the practicality of his invention: one could transmit from Europe to America, the expensive Atlantic cables became superfluous. The observatory *Cabot Tower* was built in 1897 to commemorate the anniversary of Cabot's arrival in Newfoundland. It towers above Signal Hill, which was so named because it served as an orientation point for sailors. The second canon defences on *Quidi Vidi Lake,* above the district with the same name, were also originally a French defence installations. Students in historical uniforms of the British Royal Artillery act as guides through the complex during the summer. On Water Street East, the oldest street in North America, is the *Provincial War Museum.* It preserves the memory of all of the battlefields on which Newfies fought for England with findings and descriptions. Here, exactly on this spot, Sir Humphrey is said to have founded the street and the city in 1583. A memorial plaque on the museum commemorates this.

In the summer season — and not only then — there is always something happening in St. John's, usually in the Arts & Culture Centre. Only the three most important events of the year are listed here as an illustration.

St. John's Day Celebration: a 10-day folk festival with parades, music festival, sailing and surfing regattas as well as ethnic and cultural events.

St. John's Regatta: the first Wednesday in August, North America's oldest and most famous yacht race on Quidi Vidi Lake.

Newfoundland and Labrador Annual Folk Festival: first weekend in August, a provincial festival with folk musicians, folk dancing and story tellers.

St. John's / **Accommodation**

Campsites: ''The Holdin' Ground Trailer Park,'' P.O. Box 8515, St. John's, NF A1B 3N9, Tel: (709) 368-3881, 60 places from Can$ 9. The campsite is located outside of town to the west, directly on the intersection of the Trans Canada Highway and NF Route 60, in the suburb of Donovan.

''Pippy Park Trailer Park,'' P.O. Box 8861, St. John's, NF A1B 3T2, Tel: (709) 737-3669, 132 places and for caravans and 24 for tents, from Can$ 10 (Can$ 5 for tents). The campsite is north of the city centre near the Confederation Building and the University, Nagles Place at the corner of Allandale Road. It can best be reached via the Prince Phillip Parkway.

Hotels/Motels/Bed & Breakfast: ''Sea Flow Tourist Home,'' 53-55 William Street, St. John's, NF A1C 2S3, Tel: (709) 753-2425, 4 rooms, Can$ 20, includes use of the kitchen, centrally located.

''Bird Island Guest Home,'' 150 Old Topsail Road, St. John's, NF A1E 2B1, Tel: (709) 753-4850, 2 rooms, Can$ 30.

''Fireside Guest Home,'' 28 Wicklow Street, St. John's, NF A1B 3H2, Tel: (709) 726-0237, 2 rooms, Can$ 30.

''Parkview Inn,'' 118 Military Road, St. John's, NF A1C 5N9, Tel: (709) 753-2671, 15 rooms, from Can$ 25.

''Prescott Inn Bed & Breakfast,'' 17 and 19 Military Road (two adjacent houses). ''St. John's,'' NF A1C 2C3, Tel: (709) 753-6036, 5 rooms, Can$ 39, breakfast included, non-smoking only, located centrally on the harbour.

''Kenmount Motel,'' 389 Elizabeth Avenue, St. John's, NF A1B 3P9, Tel: (709) 722-5400, 37 rooms, from Can$ 40.

''1st City Motel,'' 479 Kenmount Road, St. John's, NF A1B 3P9, Tel: (709)722-5400, 32 rooms, from Can$ 40.

There are also ten additional hotels/motels which cost Can$ 50 to 135 per night. There is no youth hostel in St. John's. The only one in Newfoundland is located in Eastport. In Newfoundland there are also no YMCA/YWCA.

St. Lawrence River

Among the countless rivers and streams in Canada, the St. Lawrence River is the most economically important. It is actually not even a river in the conventional sense. It is the "draining trench" of the Great lakes between the US and Ontario which collect the water from the rivers and streams in a massive depression. Falling off from lake to lake, the excess water seeks a way to flow out of the land which it finally does find between the Pre-Cambrian Shield to the north and the Appalachians to the south. Along its course, it takes up the water from numerous other rivers, the masses of water broaden as they flow eastwards until the mouth reaches a width of 150 km. The waters flow around the 200 kilometre long island of Anticosti before reaching the gigantic basin of the Gulf of St. Lawrence and finally the Atlantic. The abundance of fish in the brackish water and the mainland tributaries of the Gulf Banks was once considered inexhaustible. This was erroneous; the fish are meanwhile all but eliminated. The fish that remain never make it to the dinner table. They are not allowed to be served because of the high level of contamination — the government allows only the export of these fish.

The actual significance of the broad river lies in its function as the main traffic artery of the region. The developed St. Lawrence sea route can accommodate sea-going vessels up to 25,000 register tons all the way to the extremities of the Great Lakes. For this reason, some chains of hills were made passable by canals and massive locks installed to raise ships up to the level of Lake Superior. Thus, the St. Lawrence River has more significance in freight traffic than the Suez or Panama Canal.

Telegrammes and Wiring Money

In Canada, the local Canadian Pacific Railway Corporation offices as well as the Canadian National Railway Corporation offices accept telegrammes. **Telegraphic money transfers** can be also handled through the above mentioned railway offices.

Telephone

Over a thousand private companies divide the telecommunications market among themselves. The telephones accept only 25 cent coins, and, for this reason, one should always carry an ample amount of change. Calls can also be placed as a collect call or as a person-to-person call. In these cases, one merely dials '0' for operator assistance in placing the call. When calling abroad, one dials the '0' and asks for the international operator, who then places the call.

To make reservations at hotels, car rentals etc. or to obtain information from tourist offices there are special toll-free numbers beginning with 1-800.

Temperature

Temperatures are measured in Celsius in Canada. Just as often, however, the Fahrenheit thermometer is still in use. When reading the thermometer, this causes very little problem since they always have both units.

Terra Nova National Park

The Terra Nova National Park encompasses about 400 square kilometres of rocky coast and the entire island with the same name, extending into the southern end of Newfoundland's Bonavista Bay. The sub-alpine mountain landscape is distinctly divided, cut by wooded valleys and falling off to the sea at the coastal cliffs which plunge up to three hundred metres to the surf. The fully developed national park is bisected by the Trans Canadian Highway, 56 kilometres of motorway from Port Blandfort in the south to Glovertown in the North. In both towns one will find information centres run by the park administration, where one can obtain information on numerous activities and programmes offered by the park rangers.

Of the seven campsites in the park, two can be reached only on foot using the hiking paths and two more can be reached only by boat. Two park campsites with a high level of comfort on the highway (''Newman Sound Campground,'' 400 places, heated laundry facilities, coin-operated washing machines, shops etc.) and on NF Route 310 (''Malady Head Campground,'' 165 places) are subject to charge: Can$ 8 and Can$ 5.50. The former is open all year, meaning also in winter when it can be used free of charge.

A golf course, sailboat and canoe rentals make for added options alongside the broad range of outdoor activities including even deep-sea fishing out in Bonavista Bay.

Information: Superintendent Terra Nova National Park, Glovertown, NF A0G 2L0, Tel: (709) 533-2801

Time of Day

The provinces of Canada span six time zones, with only one-half hour difference between the two easternmost time zones.

Tipping

Even in the socially based country of Canada, the service personnel in restaurants and hotels receive either no wages or only a token sum. Also, service is never included in the prices! The guest at a hotel or restaurant is supposed to pay an additional sum voluntarily, appropriate to the service received. Customary in Canada are about 10% of the total price laid discretely under the plate or given directly to the service personnel. One then usually pays for the food at the central cashier.

Tourist Information

Tourism is an important basis for the Canadian economy and, for this reason, it is promoted intensively. Every small city will have an information office, the name of which varies from place to place: Visitor Information Center, Visitor Reception Bureau or Convention and Visitors' Bureau etc., but most are marked with the internationally recognised ''i.'' At these centres, one can ask specific questions and receive free brochures, information on special events, maps and so on.

In addition to this, every federal province operates an extensive information network about the region. There is always a central office and a number of branch offices on the border or in the larger cities. From the central offices, one can obtain a road map of the province free of charge, the listing of accommodation and products, making the planning stages of a trip to Canada easier.

It is essential that one's gives thought to ones inquiry and ask precisely for specific information because the selection of information is so large that information on hunting, for example, is only sent upon request.

For specific information on Canadian provinces one should contact the following addresses in Canada:

Tourism New Brunswick, P.O. Box 12345, Fredericton NB E3B 5C3, Canada, Tel: (506) 453-2377.

Tourist Services Newfoundland, Department of Development and Tourism, P.O. Box 2016, St. John's NF A1C 5R8, Tel: (709) 576-2830.

Department of Tourism Nova Scotia, P.O. Box 456, Halifax NS B3J 2R5, Canada, Tel: (902) 424-5000.

Visitor Services Prince Edward Island, P.O. Box 940, Charlottetown P.E.I. C1A 7M5, Canada, Tel: (902) 368-4444.

Traffic Regulations

The maximum speed allowed on highways (motorways) and expressways is 100 kmph; on other roads, 80 kmph; within city limits, 50 kmph and in school zones 30 kmph.

Driving under the influence of alcohol is strictly forbidden and one must always wear one's safety belt.

In some provinces one is required to drive with low-beams during the day for safety reasons. Right turns while the traffic signal is still red is allowed after initially stopping (not in Québec!). Passing school buses with red lights blinking is not permitted — not even when approaching from the opposite direction.

Transportation in Eastern Canada
Transportation in Eastern Canada / **Boats**

Those who are not departing for Canada on a holiday of horseback riding or skiing is dependent on a boat to experience the pristine nature first-hand. Wellsuited to this purpose are the Indian birch-bark canoes or a kayak, built according to those of the Inuit, made of plastic or metal. These are indispensable in exploring because of their minimal draught and weight dispersion, and therefore quite common in Canada's northern regions. If one decides on a guided water expedition, the use of paddle boats and life jackets is always included in the price.

Those who wish to explore a river or lake on their own can always rent a boat in a nearby town — and even return it elsewhere. One need not bring the boat back to where it was rented; one can return it in another town as agreed upon. These rental boats are by no means inexpensive! They are usually the widely-used open two-seat canoes, known as ''Canadians''! One will not find them under Can$ 30 per day, Can$ 150 per week or Can$ 250 for 15 days. Boat rentals can almost always be found at Hudson Bay Company locations, which can be especially recommended if one does not plan on returning the boat where it was originally rented: one can simply return it at the nearest HBC branch upon arriving at one's destination. In addition, every Natives Cooperative is capable of either renting out boats or helping one further. A good chance to have a conversation with the Indians or Inuit! And finally, the commercial agencies can be found everywhere. Those who offer outfitter services or guided tours, will also rent out boats to visitors who would prefer to explore the region on their own.

One should not count on being able to purchase an inexpensive boat second-hand — unless one is travelling at the end of the season or well before the beginning. During these times one will have no trouble purchasing a well-equipped two-seater for Can$ 100 to 150. In light of the high rental fees, one should consider buying a new boat and then selling it again mid-season. Every hardware store and department store (not only the HBC), have a selection of factory-direct boats. The length is measured in feet. The common two-seater is 19 feet in length. A 17-footer is sufficient for one person and supplies. Prices vary greatly depending on the manufacturer. The least expensive are those offered by Woolworth; a 17-footer can be had for under Can$ 500.

The boat can be resold at the end of one's trip to another traveller at a camp-site, by advertising in the classified section of newspapers or on the radio. There are also bulletin boards in every post office and department store serving this very purpose. Another option just as effective and inexpensive is to bring along a portable or inflatable boat from ones home country. Those who own a collapsible boat or inflatable canoe should definitely consider bringing it. The prohibitive fees for overweight luggage do not always permit this. This is the only way, however, to be certain one will be able to bring a boat along in the bush taxis.

Transportation in Eastern Canada / **Bush Taxi**

In Canada's northern regions, the role played by the taxi is taken over by the light aircraft — the bush taxi. One will find a plane whose services can be hired even in the most remote villages in the wilderness. In summer they start and land on pontoons; in winter on skis. They are able to land on any lake large enough.

Among these light aircrafts are every type and every make. The two which have become standard for the taxi service are the smaller Cessna 180/185 with room for two passengers and luggage and the Beaver which seats four with room for luggage. The cost of such a taxi ride can be calculated in advance. The service is charged in miles. The cost is calculated for the exact flight distance and then doubled! This is because the costs for the return flight, although empty, must also be covered. This is then multiplied by the base price of Can\$ 2 or 4.24 (Beaver) per mile. High in the north, one must count on prices up to 10% higher. As a rule one pays before starting the trip. If the pilot began the flight but was unable to complete it for unforeseen reasons, then one need not pay for the second attempt. As the distances in the expanses of the north are often underestimated by newcomers, it is expressly stated here that one can only fly inexpensively if one drives to the airport nearest the destination and hires a pilot there. Luggage should be as light as possible due to the limited stowage space.

Transportation in Eastern Canada / **Railway**

The few railways in Canada are run by private companies. Actually the only significant railway route in Canada is the one from Halifax on the Atlantic to Vancouver on the Pacific. A number of regional companies operate a few north-south routes branching off of the Trans Canada route. Of these, the most interesting to tourists is the passenger route from Vancouver via Prince Rupert to Jasper/Banff operated by BC-Railway.

	min. validity	CANRAILPASS	YOUTH* CANRAILPASS
entire railway system (max. 30 days)	15 days	299/9	239/5
between Winnipeg and Atlantic (max. 15 days)	8 days	189/9	159/5
between Winnipeg and the Pacific (max. 15 days)	8 days	199/9	169/5
Maritimes, Nova Scotia, Prince Edward Island, New Brunswick (max. 15 days)	8 days	99/9	65/5

The prices after the slash are for each additional day.

*The YOUTHCANRAIL PASS is valid for young people from 12-24 years of age. Children under 12 pay half of the adult fare.

The various categories defined by different railroad companies is not of significance for travellers because passenger travel is organized through VIA Rail Canada Inc., 2 Place Ville-Marie, Montréal (Québec) H3B 2G6.

There are tourist passes available for the entire Canadian railroad network, making a long trip through Canada affordable.

Transportation in Eastern Canada / **Flight Pass**

Air travel is often a necessity in Canada considering the distances involved. One will soon realise that, within Canada, a state-run airline cartel determines the extremely expensive fares. One should, however, note that it is much less expensive to book a domestic flight in Canada from Europe.

In addition, there are also discounts for travelling by air to a number of destinations which brings down the price of air travel considerably. These are similarly structured to the VIA-Canrail-Pass *(→Railway)*. Because the terms and conditions for these passes are constantly changing, the following example with the ''Atlantic Canadapass'' offered by Air Nova (a partner of Air Canada) is intended only as an illustration.

With this pass, one can fly to destinations within the four Atlantic provinces in a triangle between Goose Bay (Labrador) in the north, Fredericton (New Brunswick) in the south and St. John's (Newfoundland) in the east.

The prices are staggered according to the number of destinations desired. Six destinations, for example, cost Can$ 399, meaning that the three above mentioned and three additional cities could be visited at an incredibly cheap price. Or said differently: the sizable distances can be travelled for about £ 35 (US$ 60)!

Those who would like to fly inexpensively should definitely book well in advance from their home country.

Transportation in Eastern Canada / **Greyhound Bus**

In North America, the Greyhound Bus is the only means of transportation with which one can reach cross-country destinations. The railway routes are far too few and a city which is not included in the bus network can only be reached by private car — or possibly by plane.

Although the Greyhound buses look alike in Canada and the US, the two companies are operated independent of each other — even hopelessly at odds. the reason for this is an company-wide strike within the US company, hardly noticable to the passengers. All the US Greyhound buses are driven by strike-breakers because the company fired all of the striking employees. In the US all routes are in full operation. This is not the case in Canada. The Canadian Greyhound company is labour oriented and no longer serves routes in the United States. The buses serving the routes Seattle — Vancouver, Chicago — Winnipeg and Montréal — Boston or New York are no longer admitted to Canadian bus terminals and no bus tickets are sold in the United States. In Winnipeg, for instance, the US-route departs and terminates at the VIA Rail train station. Passengers must then take a taxi to the Canadian bus terminal 2 kilometres away.

What is even more aggrivating is that the Canadian company has discontinued all other cooperation with the US company. In Canada, the Ameripass, the inexpensive bus pass, is no longer accepted. It is only valid on the three US-Canadian routes mentioned above, which are served by US buses. Those who wish to travel from the east to the west inexpensively must then do so south of the US-Canadian border, for example, from New York to Seattle. The Ameripass is available in a number of travel agencies worldwide. They have even become less expensive than in the past.

4-day pass	£ 45 (US$ 80)
7-day pass	£ 85 (US$ 150)
15-day pass	£ 120 (US$ 212)
30-day pass	£ 150 (US$ 265)

Please note that these prices are approximate and subject to change. They are only valid when the passes are purchased outside the US. Within the US, they are up to 70% more expensive!

Within the Canadian company, there are different names of the buslines from region to region, but which all belong to the central Greyhound company in terms of majority shareholdings. These are "Voyageur" in Québec, "SMT" in New Brunswick, "Terra Transport" in Newfoundland, and "Acadian Line" in Nova Scotia. The Greyhound passes and tickets are not valid for buses run by other companies in individual cities and regions. This is also true of the cities where buses are the main form of regional and innermetropolitan transportation.

Travel Documents

Entering Canada should not cause any problems for most nationalities. Citizens of EC member states may enter with a valid passport and need no visa. Visitor status lasts six months and can be extended a further six months upon request. One must prove that one has sufficient funds to cover expenses while in Canada. Presenting a credit card will be of help in taking care of this formality. The return trip must also be confirmed (by showing a ticket for the return flight, for instance). Those who plan on staying for more than three months will need to apply for permission to do so.

For US citizens any valid form of identification will suffice when entering Canada. Regulations for citizens of Great Britain, Australia and New Zealand are similarly uncomplicated.

Persons under 18 years of age travelling alone should be able to present a document stating that they are permitted by their legal guardians to be travelling alone.

Certification of vaccinations are not required at present.

Travellers from the United States and Europe can bring their automobiles into the country duty-free for 12 months. However, due to epidemic control regulations, it is required that the car go through a special cleaning process. This is taken care of by the shipping companies.

A national driving licence from Europe or the United States is sufficient to meet Canadian requirements; however, one can also obtain an international driving licence at the Department of Motor Vehicles for a small fee. Vehicle registration from one's home country is also sufficient in Canada. It is a different story with automobile insurance, however. European insurance usually only covers claims within Europe. Therefore, one must ask one's insurance company for information and supplement the coverage if necessary. Another option is to take out term liability insurance in Canada. This is, however, only possible when done in one's home country.

Travelling to Eastern Canada
Travelling to Eastern Canada / **By Air**

British Airways offers flights to Montréal for £ 390 (US$690) (peak season) and £ 949 (US$545) (off-season) from London. The prices quoted are, however, valid only Monday to Thursday. On other days of the week, one must count on a surcharge.

Some airlines (Air Canada, for instance) offer special fares for young people between the ages of 12 and 21 as well as students between 22 and 25.

The leading international airport in Eastern Canada is the one in Halifax, Nova Scotia. Here, one has good access to the excellent domestic air travel network in Canada. One important factor is to book and pay for flights in one's home country. In Canada, the tickets can be up to 40% more expensive than in Europe, for instance.

A number of other airports are the destinations of direct international flights as well; for example, St. John's and Gardner in Newfoundland. These are often destinations for direct flights from London.

The two international airports in Montréal are called "Dorval" and "Mirabel." Aérocar buses operate between these airports and also offer transportation into the city. From Dorval into the city, one must expect to pay Can\$ 7; from Mirabel, Can\$ 9.

The airport in Halifax is called "Dartmouth International Airport," (P.O. Box 470, Dartmouth, NS B2Y 2Y8, Tel: (902) 427-5500) and is located about 25 kilometres outside the city. There is no means of public transportation from the city to the airport. The trip by airport shuttle bus costs Can\$ 10 from downtown Halifax; Can\$ 17 return trip. The buses offer this shuttle service from 6 am to 10 pm to the larger hotels in Halifax and Dartmouth. They will also make stops upon request. More detailed information is available through: Airport Transfer Ltd., 71 Simmonds Drive, Dartmouth, NS B3B 1N7, Tel: (902) 456-3100.

Those continuing to another destination within Canada can use the VIA Rail passenger trains. The train station is located in the northern part of downtown Halifax, 1161 Hollis Street, Halifax, NS B3H 2P6, Tel: (902) 429-8421. From here, the Trans-Canada Express sets off on its journey across the continent to Vancouver every two days. One can also continue the journey by bus with the Greyhound lines partner in Nova Scotia: Acadian Lines Ltd., 6040 Almon Street, Halifax, NS B3K 1T8, Tel: (902) 454-9321. The bus terminal is in the northwestern part of downtown Halifax on the corner of Robie Street and Almon Street (→ *Transportation in Eastern Canada).*